The Roundabouts of Life

A Journey of a Soul on a Mission

Marlon Bobier Vargas, SVD

with an introduction by
Adam MacDonald, SVD

with foreword by
Steve Bevans, SVD, and Jerry Orbos, SVD

edited by Theresa Carson

Copyright © 2020 by Marlon Bobier Vargas, SVD
All rights reserved. This book or any portion thereof may not be reproduced or used in any manner whatsoever without the express written permission of the publisher except for the use of brief quotations in a book review.

Printed in the United States of America

First Printing, 2020

ISBN 978-0-578-72570-3

Cover art by Canva
Cover design by Theresa Carson and Khanh Ha, SVD

In gratitude to

my family

and to

my brothers and sisters in the Arnoldus Family:

the Society of the Divine Word (SVD),

the Missionary Sister Servants of the Holy Spirit (SSpS),

and the

Servants of the Holy Spirit of Perpetual Adoration (SSpSAP)

Featured on this page is an icon by Fr. Guerric Llanes, a Trappist monk of the Abbey of New Clairvaux in Vina, California. In addition to serving his monastic community as vocation and novice director, he has been learning both theoretical and practical aspects of traditional Byzantine iconography. The icon of Holy Fatherhood Lord Sabaoth reflects God's oneness in three persons and calls to mind Saint Arnold's prayer: "May the holy and triune God lead you more and more into the basic mystery of his divine love."

"Life is a mosaic. Humans are made up of broken pieces and are God's masterpieces." With these words, Father Marlon Bobier Vargas, SVD, fashions a creative mosaic of his own life's stories and spiritual journeys. He shows how "change is a relentless reality," as God makes a masterpiece of our human twists and turns. I kept reading the chapters of this book, marveling at the depth of insight and the clarity of expression Marlon brings to life. This is a beautiful tribute to grace. Inspired by the writings of Saint Arnold Jansen, SVD founder, Marlon does the SVD missioners proud.

Richard N. Fragomeni, Ph.D.
Professor of Liturgy and Preaching
Catholic Theological Union

The reflections of Marlon Vargas reveal a man who seeks to learn whatever he can from experiences of life, ordinary and extraordinary alike. The exercise of such a habit of thought can only enhance the ministerial efficacy he is in the process of developing. As he continues in this manner of thought it will lead him into ever deeper theological reflection on life itself.

Dianne Bergant, CSA
Carroll Stuhlmueller, CP, Distinguished Professor Emerita of Old Testament Studies at Catholic Theological Union

To read these reflections is to join Marlon on a journey whose geographical span includes Philippines, United States and Spain. However, this is much more a pilgrimage into the heart of God, into the heart of one's self, into the heart of encounter with the neighbor near and far. It is a missionary journey, it is a camino. Filled with gentleness and honesty, profundity and humor, hope and love, you will find wisdom from the lives of Saint Arnold Janssen and seeker Marlon Bobier Vargas. Read, reflect, and buen camino!

> **Maria Cimperman, RSCJ**
> Associate Professor & Director of the
> Center for the Study of Consecrated
> Life at Catholic Theological Union

Through sharing experiences of his encounters with the Divine Word, Marlon moves readers to discover the pervasive presence of God in their own lives. This story of a vocation draws us into the larger saga of salvation where we, along with all of creation, are initiated into the unfolding mission of God who is Love. The sun rises and trees touch for the glory of God; so we can practice presence, embody compassion, and receive communion in community. Readers will find in these pages diverse and practical invitations to respond to the Word in the Spirit that will reward their reflection through the seasons of liturgy and life. Marlon teaches us to live into the blessings of God's goodness prepared for us in times of joy and suffering, waiting and longing, serving and celebrating so that we might become part of the story of Jesus "read" by those we meet in our lives.

> **Anne McGowan, Ph.D.**
> Assistant Professor of Liturgy
> Catholic Theological Union

Whether they are challenging times or ordinary days, the human search for meaning, can lead the seeker to the ultimate question, "Where is God in all of this anyway?" With transparency and vulnerability, Marlon Bobier Vargas, SVD, offers a simple way into the question in order to discover a deeper meaning. He invites the reader to listen in as he shares personal experiences that led him to discover God's presence in every situation and circumstance of his life. Marlon is a worthy and wise companion for any seeker who ventures down this path of intimate discovery.

Connie Schoen, OP
Dominican Sister of Peace
Program Director
Religious Formation Conference

Marlon Vargas offers his own personal journey in a series of vignettes that gives a glimpse of God's face through the various people and situations he encounters as a missionary for the Society of the Divine Word (SVD). Truly a man after the heart of SVD founding-father, Saint Arnold Janssen, Marlon imbibes his founder's missionary spirit in order to bring the light of Christ's Gospel to all. Any aspiring missionary will find something worthwhile in it to ponder upon and take as a guide for their own journey.

Guerric Ariel Llanes, OCSO
Monk of the Abbey of New Clairvaux

It is an easily readable odyssey of faith and a pilgrimage toward committed service to others.

> **James McCarthy**
> SPRED Founder and Director
> Special Religious Developmental
> Ministry (SPRED) of the
> Archdiocese of Chicago

The Roundabouts of Life: A Journey of a Soul on a Mission is a fine reflection on the lived experience of Marlon Bobier Vargas, SVD, as he follows his path to growth in faith and service to others with courage and joy. I enjoyed both his narrative and writing style.

> **Mary Therese Harrington, SH**
> Co-director of Special Religious
> Development Ministry (SPRED)
> of the Archdiocese of Chicago

Marlon is on the search for happiness. Early on Marlon asks the question "Who is the loving God, the Father?" We belong to the same SPRED group of *friends* (people with different developmental and intellectual abilities). In this experience and in Marlon's other stories, it is in the experience of friendship when we find ourselves being happy to be together and when that happens the Father is with us. He is brave and engaging."

> **Kitty Hartigan**
> SPRED Ministry Catechist

This book is about a young man named Marlon Bobier Vargas as he journeys through life as a pilgrim. The journey begins with Marlon search for something more in his self-identity, then continues with his search for something more as a Christian, and now Marlon is on an everyday search for something more as the Holy Spirit invites him to fuller service in the Church. If you are searching for "something more" this book will be a big help to your discernment process as you too make the same pilgrimage of life that Marlon is journeying along as he listens for the whisperings of the Spirit.

William Seifert, SVD
Divine Word Missionary
Techny, Illinois, USA

Small pieces of a story that will undoubtedly inspire many other stories along the way.

It is not the number of miles you walk with someone that makes encounters more or less meaningful. True encounters can happen at any roundabouts of life. It was Duenas, Spain, one of those roundabouts that allowed me to get to know Marlon, in the context of our Arnoldus Family program. Meeting Marlon again at CTU allowed me to discover in Marlon a person with deep longings to serve God in the missionary vocation.

I am impressed by the depths of Marlon's reflections. They emerge from personal life situations that flow through his inner sacred space, where he allows every single life event to be transformed and shaped by the Love of God. From his inner being, like little pieces of art, these reflections can reach all corners of the world, to all ages and life realities. His words can become meaningful moments in the roundabouts of other people's life.

At a time when the coronavirus (COVID-19) has all of humanity under threat, isolation, and fear, Marlon's significant life experiences shared in this Collection are precious pearls that reveal an unshakable Hope and Trust in God who Loves and Cares for every human being.

Are you searching for a deeper meaning in life or longing for something greater? Marlon's stories will draw you into your own experiences of life, as you travel through the pages of this collection. His stories will lead you to get connected to your inner sources. They can open up your treasure and provide ways to revisit the life events of your Journey. They can inspire and impel you to search for your contribution to making our world a better place. You will be surprised by what these stories can offer to you.

Lidia Kunze, SSpS
Misiones, Argentina
April 6, 2020

Table of Contents

Preface i

Foreword iv

Introduction 1

God's work in progress 4

Witnessing God's mercy in ministry 9

Home: Where a missionary's journey begins 13

Home: Renewing family relationships 17

Trees planted by streams: Seeing God's grace in the arbor 20

Social challenge: The gifts and tasks of learning a language 24

God's peculiar grace 29

The earthen vessels of Parroquia Nuestra Señora de Altagracia 33

The quest and the questions 37

The backpack 40

A journey through nature 43

'Buen camino!' A greeting of connection and friendship 45

The end and beginning of the grace-filled journey 48

An Emmaus journey in Niebla 52

Working with the saints next door 56

Christ's compassionate heart 59

Faithful friends: Rooted in Jesus 63

Generation Z and spiritual companions 67

Presence in sacred waiting 72

Art of waiting for busy people 75

Hearing Christ's coming through our beating hearts 79

How liturgy and worship fostered my religious missionary vocation 82

Let our children come to us 85

The excellence of love 88

A marathon, a faith journey and the abounding grace of God 92

Emotional memory of God 96

Sharing sacred space with the marginalized 100

The joy, beauty and goodness of Christ's peace 105

Have courage, wash one another's feet! 110

To hold fast to the life that fosters faith, charity, and hope in time of pandemic 114

Saint Arnold Janssen, SVD (1837-1909) 118

Acknowledgments 121

Preface

More likely than not, you and I have met before. Somewhere along the road our paths crossed knowingly or unknowingly, directly or indirectly. If not, you are reading this book, and we are connected right now.

We are both passing through the spiritual roundabout of life. It is a shared pathway. Like in actual roundabouts, our lives encounter a topsy-turvy direction. There are many turns that can lead us to entrances and exits, to upward and downward routes that evoke mixed and overwhelming emotions; that present to us transforming life experiences.

When I decided to discern my vocation and responded to the call of becoming a Divine Word Missionary, I ventured into a spiritual roundabout. It is a pilgrimage path—an expedition and an adventure. I underwent a formation process that led me to re-discover myself. I struggled with many and unexpected transitions in life. I encountered different pilgrims along the journey: fellow missionaries, married couples, professionals, the young and old, the educated and uneducated, able-bodied and disabled, free and imprisoned, religious and secular, individuals and communities.

I strived to adjust and adapt with constancy, spontaneity, and flexibility. I learned from tough decision-making. I found myself sometimes in a chaotic condition. I persevered to stay on top of everything. Through my interactions with different people, I experienced God's tremendous grace.

I share with you this book that contains a collection of reflections and stories about my experiences as a religious missionary. To be honest, this book is not the kind of material that I planned to publish. But the experiences on my faith journey transpired very differently and unfolded in ways far beyond what I had expected.

The roundabouts of life involve passing through an unchartered territory where our trust in God is challenged. For instance, many of us were scared, worried, and anxious when the COVID-19 pandemic came to us. We were forced to move away from a state or a condition with which we were familiar, and we entered into and explored a new region that was unknown to us. That required us to take gradual and careful steps. So we are in an in-between moment. We are in a time between times on our journey, a time where we are leaving one place but not yet arriving at a new place. We are standing in the middle of a juncture of significant change.

I was in awe and wonder when I spent time reviewing my journals. From all my written reflections, I deliberately and prayerfully selected the reflection articles included in this book. I found myself immersed in God's warm presence and dynamic movement not only in my own life but more importantly in the lives of people I met along the way. It is my hope that you will be inspired by stories about my encounters with different people—old and new friends—during my stay in the United States, in Spain, and in the Philippines. These sacred encounters happened in parishes, SVD communities, hospitals, prisons, schools, and other places where people entered and exited the roundabout of life.

In a special way, this book is meant to honor and thank the many people who accompanied me and taught me about the living God who is present with us, who acts with love and mercy, and in whose hands is control over chaos.

While we live in this in-between situation, we are called to go and make disciples of all nations. We are in challenging times and yet there are rewarding occasions that call us to rejuvenate our sense of identity and transform our relationships with one another. We are called to reflect on the values and beliefs that give our lives meaning.

At the end of each chapter is a quote from Saint Arnold Janssen, our founder. I borrowed these quotes from the book *God's Holy Will Alone* by Divine Word Missionary Friedbert Ewertz translated by Rudy Heckel, SVD, in the hope that they will be truly inspiring. Every quote is followed by a few questions that might help you as a reader to reflect on God's presence and movement in your own life.

It is my hope that, as you read each chapter, you will be able to relate, reflect, recognize, and appreciate your own life-transforming and grace-filled experiences of God's love.

Our almighty and loving God creates unceasingly a wonderful mosaic out of our lives. God shapes and forms us by guiding us through our ongoing life experiences.

Through God, with God, and in God, we're able to embrace our unique giftedness by accepting what God offers us. It urges us to trust with hope throughout the journey.

May you find in this book an indescribable sense of God-given gratitude, joy, and hope.

Foreword

GRACE IN THE MOMENT

In the eighteenth century, the simple priest and spiritual director Jean Pierre de Caussade coined the phrase "the sacrament of the present moment." Every moment, every person we see, every experience we have, can be—if we have eyes to see and a heart to feel—a revelation of God's presence and love. Such an idea was expressed as well by the twentieth-century French novelist Georges Bernanos in the closing lines of his classic *Diary of a Country Priest: All is Grace*.

It is this spirituality and this wisdom that struck me as I read the short reflections offered here by Marlon Vargas, my former student and SVD confrere. None of these reflections speak of earth-shaking moments in Marlon's life, and yet each one begins from an incident or experience in which Marlon has seen the presence of God's grace: walking on the Camino on the ancient pilgrimage route towards Santiago de Compostela, meeting his estranged father, chatting with a friend on Facebook, coming home after several years abroad, learning Spanish, taking leave of people in a parish, contemplating bare trees. All these experiences are, for Marlon, sacraments. All are signs of grace.

Several of these reflections are also eminently practical. Wisdom is gleaned from spending time in a small village in Spain, from contemplating the saints on All Saints' Day, reflecting on how to spend a meaningful Advent. These are the reflections of a youthful, enthusiastic mind and heart, and I for one hope that they continue to deepen and grow as Marlon sets out on the journey of a lifetime in ministry.

Marlon never lets us forget that he is a Divine Word Missionary, a son, as it were, of St. Arnold Janssen, SVD "Father, Leader, and Founder," as we find inscribed on his tomb in Steyl, Holland. Every reflection in this little book ends with words of Fr. Arnold, and they are always words that connect with Marlon's reflection on the presence of grace in the daily experiences of his life. And we are not let off the hook either. Each reflection asks us questions that lead us to a personal reflection on the grace present in our own lives.

As I understand it, Marlon offers these reflections to friends on the occasion of his ordination to the priesthood. May their honesty, simplicity, eloquence, and vulnerability be a pledge of Marlon's own honesty, simplicity, eloquence, and vulnerability as he grows into this ministry of discipleship and service.

Fr. Steve Bevans, SVD
Divine Word Theologate
Chicago, IL, USA
February 17, 2020

Life is a journey, and the most important journey in life is not so much our career, nor our financial, nor our popularity journey, but our journey to the heart – to God's heart, to other persons' hearts, and to our very own hearts.

"The Roundabouts of Life" {A Journey of a Soul on a Mission} by Marlon Bobier Vargas, SVD, is an honest, heartwarming account of a young man's journey towards meaning, calling, and mission. Reading it is a *"cor ad cor loquitor"* experience—a heart speaking to a heart.

The author is impressive, but more than that, he is expressive. His honesty and simplicity has led me deeper into my own spirituality, which I call Moments Spirituality – i.e., that God speaks to us in the most simple moments of our lives. Yes, there is always something or someone there to remind us of His living and loving presence as we journey on.

I thank the author for his courage to share not only the ideas of his head, nor just the work of his hands, but also the love in his heart. And I am particularly thankful to the author for making our SVD Founder St. Arnold Janssen come alive and become relevant in this our present day and time, thus making the Heart of Jesus live in the hearts of all!

Fr. Jerry M. Orbos, SVD
Christ the King Seminary
Quezon City, Philippines
April 18, 2020

Introduction

"When are you leaving?" "How long are you here for?" "For how long will you be with us?" These are just some of the questions I get asked on a regular basis as a vocation director every time my frequent travels bring me home to my local Divine Word Missionary community.

But as frequently as I hear these questions, there's another query that echoes in my ears and penetrates my heart every time I hear it: "How many fish did you catch?" Now it's easy enough for me to understand where the question comes from; after all, as a vocation director, I am, using the words of Scripture, a proverbial "fisher of men."

But unlike the questions I get about the length of my stay and visits with the community, this one isn't as easy to answer! The truth is, how do I really know for certain that I've "caught a fish?" Is it the first time they respond to my call, text, or email? Is it when they consent to getting together for lunch or a cup of coffee? Is it when they make a "Come and See" visit to our community? Is it when they apply for our formation program? Is it when they get accepted? Is it when they arrive for their first day of seminary formation? Is it when they profess First Vows? Or is it when they profess Perpetual Vows or get ordained as a deacon or priest? The simple fact of the matter is that, there's just no knowing for certain which of these moments is the one when God's call to a religious vocation has been answered once and for all!

Although the ministry of a vocation director is full of uncertainties when it comes to seeing the fruits of one's labor, it's clear that the focus of the work is twofold: promoting awareness of religious life and the specific charism of the community a vocation director represents, and then accompanying on the journey of discernment those who've heard God's call and are seeking to respond. And thus the "success" in vocation ministry is found not so much in the numbers of those who enter religious life but in the fidelity to these efforts at promotion and accompaniment.

In my nearly nine years of experience as vocation director for the Divine Word Missionary community, I have been richly blessed with much joy and fulfillment in committing my time and energy to this most noble endeavor! And the fact of the matter is that, by the grace of God and the work of the Holy Spirit, I've been humbled again and again by the young men who boldly and courageously offer their lives to be used by God as instruments of his love and mercy in the lives of others, several of whom have now become my Divine Word Missionary confreres!

One of those confreres has a story uniquely his own. Marlon Vargas was teaching at a Catholic school on the island of Guam when he saw an ad for our Divine Word community as part of a search engine marketing campaign we had launched through Facebook and Google+. Clicking on the ad and submitting a request for further information, Marlon soon received an email from yours truly, inviting him to learn more about who we are and what we do as missionaries of the Word of God to the world and its peoples.

These initial exchanges led to a series of extended conversations during which I learned that Marlon had been discerning his God-given gifts for a number of years and that if he in fact felt called to discern with the Divine Word Missionaries, we would not only have something to offer him in terms of further education, a spiritual formation program, and a community of like-minded individuals, but we as a community would be enriched by all that Marlon would bring to us: his intelligence, his compassion, his dedication, and the seriousness with which he desires to give his life to God!

As you will read in these chapters, Marlon's is a soul who is on a mission. And it's clear that that mission commenced long before Marlon ever knew what a Divine Word Missionary is. It's likewise certain that Marlon's journey continues to unfold and that he will spend the rest of his life growing in the awareness of being created in the image and likeness of God, being transformed by the power of God's grace, and seeking to serve as an instrument of the ongoing transformation of our world.

As you learn more about the journey of Marlon's soul in the pages that follow, I invite you to accept the invitation to consider the journey of your own soul as a child of God and what is the plan and purpose of God in your life both now and in the future. After all, like Marlon, as members of the baptized faithful, each and every one of us shares in the universal call to holiness. Where is your journey leading you? What will be the next chapters you allow God to write in your life?

Please join me in thanking Marlon for allowing us to be witnesses to the work of God in his life and likewise for allowing God to use Marlon as a witness of his love in each of our lives. May Marlon be richly blessed as he receives the Sacrament of Holy Orders and is ordained a priest of Jesus Christ ordained to serve the people of God for the rest of his days.

May the darkness of sin and the night of unbelief vanish before the Light of the Word and the Spirit of Grace, and may the heart of Jesus live in the hearts of all.

Praised be Jesus Christ. Now and forever. Amen!

Fr. Adam MacDonald, SVD
Vocation Director
March 18, 2020

God's work in progress

On the first day of my novitiate formation year, I spent the night at the bedside of a dying man. One of the Divine Word priests was dying. As is the tradition in the Society of the Divine Word, I stayed with the priest so the elderly man would not be alone when he died.

I kept vigil for three nights. On the third morning, I spoke to him even though I had no way of knowing if he heard me. I told him, "I'm scared because I'm facing another stage of my formation. When you meet Him, please tell Him that I'm Marlon the novice, and I want to become...." Before I finished, he took a deep breath, opened his eyes, looked at me and passed away.

A few days later, I struggled with my emotions at the burial. Another Divine Word Missionary recognized my distress and spoke to me. He walked with me around the cemetery and introduced me to priests and brothers buried there.

That experience moved me and brought back memories of my difficult childhood. My family lived in poverty. My father abandoned us even before I was old enough to have a memory of him. I questioned the image of a loving father.

When I was five years old, my mother married my stepfather. By age six, I began helping to support the family. At the time, one day seemed to merge into the next. I went to school, came home, slept and then sold produce at a local flea market from midnight until 8 a.m. before starting the cycle again. When I was older, I again dealt with the question of why other children lived relatively carefree lives while I experienced poverty. After high school, I felt deprived of a childhood and left my family. I went to college. They were very tough times becoming independent as a teenager, but I thought, "I don't want to live my life in this situation."

I built a new life. I earned a bachelor's degree in religious education and guidance counseling from the University of Santo Tomas in Manila and a master's degree in special education from the University of the Philippines in Quezon City. I give honor to the generous people who made scholarships available and institutions where I have worked.

At different times, the call to the consecrated religious life entered my mind. When I was young, I was attracted to serving at Mass. After high school, I thought about entering religious life but was not ready. While at college, I received an admittance letter from a religious order even though I had not applied. I have been influenced by several religious orders—the Salesians in grade school and high school, the Dominicans in college, and the Claretians and Jesuits in my professional life. I taught high school at the Jesuit-run Ateneo de Manila, one of the most prestigious schools in the Philippines.

During the First Asian Mission Congress in 2006 held in Chiang Mai, Thailand, Cardinal Luis Antonio Tagle (who at that time was the bishop of Imus, Cavite, in the Philippines and now the prefect of the Congregation for the Evangelization of Peoples) spoke and called the participants to tell and retell the story of Jesus. That's when I discovered my missionary calling.

For the next five years, I served God as a lay minister and was involved with World Youth Day, Asian Youth Day and National Youth Day. Youth ministry was my passion. I love inspiring others through my stories and encouraging them to go to God. But, there came a time when my heart called me to do something else. In 2011, I longed for something more. I decided that I would leave the Philippines under one of three conditions: to study, teach religion or become a missionary.

It was then that I received an invitation to teach at Santa Barbara Catholic School in Guam, a small island in the Pacific Ocean. I enjoyed island life—the slower pace, nature and outdoor activities. Yet, I was still longing for something more.

One day at Mass when the presider prayed the Eucharistic prayer, I realized that I wanted to serve as a priest. It was as if someone whispered to me, "Yes, Marlon, you are serving me as a lay minister, but I want you to serve me as a priest."

I browsed the Internet and came upon the Society of the Divine Word's Facebook page. After meeting Vocation Director Adam MacDonald, I accepted an invitation to a come-and-see visit at Techny, Illinois, and attended the 2012 SVD priesthood ordination.

Later that year, I joined the Society of the Divine Word and began theological studies at Catholic Theological Union in Chicago. When I finished my associate year, I did my Clinical Pastoral Education at New York University Langone Medical Center, where I ministered to the aging, sick and dying.

In August 2013, I started my first year of novitiate. Novitiate was an experience of Jesus at his Transfiguration. It led me to know Jesus more deeply, love Him intimately, and follow Him more closely.

One of the life-changing events that occurred during my novitiate was getting to know my biological father. I received news from my mother that she had obtained my father's contact information. I do not have words to describe my first ever long-distance phone conversation with my father.

I learned that I had been living with incomplete knowledge about myself. He called me his son and apologized. Although the experience was healing, it challenged my sense of identity. For 32 years, I carried around information about myself that was not true.

I chose to step back and work through my issues. After two years in novitiate, I professed first vows on August 8, 2015.

My incompleteness is my reality. I want to help others feel complete. I cherish being a Divine Word Missionary. The support of Divine Word priests and brothers, sharing their wisdom and life experiences, has helped me find answers to my question, "Who is the loving God the Father?" It's part of my identity—to be a part a of something.

Now I have a sense of wholeness and belonging. Looking back, I realize that it was all part of God's plan. At the time of my profession of vows, I was working on a mosaic for an amateur exhibit. It led me to the profound insight that life is really about God. Life is a mosaic. Humans are made up of broken pieces, and we are God's masterpieces.

Meaningful life experiences and the people whom we meet on the journey are the canvas of God's mosaic. God is arranging the pieces into a masterpiece. Brokenness, incompleteness, imperfections—God wants us to continue working to become works of art.

Words from Saint Arnold Janssen
"The temple of our heart is wonderfully built by a divine master hand."

For reflection
- Have you experienced a sense that God is calling you to "something more"?
- What are you doing to answer that call?

Witnessing God's mercy in ministry

In Spring semester of 2016, I resumed my ministry at the University of Chicago Medical Center filled with a grateful and hopeful spirit. I knew that my chaplaincy ministry would be one-of-a-kind and relevant because of two special and significant occasions in the Catholic Church: the Jubilee Year of Mercy and the Lenten season. I'm inspired by my ministry of bringing the spirit of God's mercy, compassion, forgiveness, and healing to those who are sick, ill and dying.

Despite this joy, my first week was deeply sad. Three of the elder members of the Society of the Divine Word—two brothers and one priest—passed away. During my novitiate years, I ministered to them, providing them assistance in their weak and less-abled conditions.

I developed very deep and special relationships with each of them as a confrere, brother, mentor and friend. We shared many moments together, such as eating at the same table, playing Bingo, exploring Chicago and sharing stories about their mission experiences.

I witnessed their struggles in trying to live each day with joy, love and hope. I am sad that they're gone but am glad that they are resting eternally in peace with our loving God. And I am thankful that I have wonderful and loving memories of them. They lived lives of service.

Serving others is a fulfilling way to begin the Lenten season. As a chaplain, I took ashes to several Catholic patients, staff and visitors in the hospital on Ash Wednesday. At first, I felt anxious.

I was nervous about people's reactions when I offered ashes to them. I worried that they might not want to receive ashes, that patients—with their debilitating health conditions—were not really interested in practicing Church rituals at that time of suffering. I thought that their suffering situation might have lessened, if not taken, their faith in God.

But, I was wrong. I was surprised by people's responses during my visits. When I walked towards one patient's room, a couple approached me and asked where they could receive ashes. I realized that the couple saw the mark of a cross on my forehead, which led them to approach me.

We went to the side of the hallway, and I led them in prayer. I sensed their joy when I imposed the sign of the cross in ashes on their foreheads.

Then, I encountered another couple in the first room visitation. As I entered the room, the husband was standing by his wife's bedside. They welcomed me with wonderful smiles.

They accepted my invitation to pray together Pope Francis' prayer for the extraordinary Jubilee Year of Mercy. As I read the prayer, I was struck by the words, "You willed that your ministers would also be clothed in weakness in order that they may feel compassion for those in ignorance and error: let everyone who approaches them feel sought after, loved, and forgiven by God...."

Feeling humbled and privileged at that moment, I ministered to the couple. I felt gratitude because I believe that God used me to bring His compassion to the couple, most especially to the wife who had just had major surgery. When I said the words "let everyone who approaches them (the ministers) feel sought after, loved, and forgiven by God," tears flow down her cheek.

Perhaps she felt God's love and mercy at that moment. I stayed for a bit and conversed with them about Jesus' parables of the lost coin and the prodigal son. I encouraged the patient to continue her meditation on Jesus' Gospel because it is a powerful and transforming way of experiencing God's comfort and healing.

I hesitated to enter the final patient's room. From outside, I saw a young lady sitting on a chair with a bandage wrapped around her head. Her parents stood next to her, talking. The lights were off, and the curtains were closed, making the room a bit dark. I conquered my hesitation and approached the family inside the room. After making the sign of the cross with ashes on their foreheads, I encourage them to make their present family condition a time for a Lenten journey with Christ, the God who is with them in the midst of their suffering. Again, I saw tears flowing from the mother's eyes. I was touched by the father's words, "Thank you so much for passing by. We greatly appreciate it."

Reflection upon the death of my three dear Divine Word confreres has led me to become more deeply attuned to the season of Lent. The physical bodies of my friends soon will become dust. Yet, their deaths are not a meaningless end of life but rather celebrations of meaningful lives as Divine Word Missionaries.

A passage from Megan McKenna's book *"Lent: Reflections and Stories in the Daily Readings"* came to mind: "They are connected to death, the cross, and suffering—the suffering and our share of the burden of the cross that is a necessary response to the unnecessary suffering, death, and injustice rampant in our world."

I kept this thought in mind and heart when I marked ashes and uttered the words with hope: "Remember, you are dust and to dust you will return." My visit to the hospital on Ash Wednesday has led me to an intimate experience and profound appreciation of God's mercy through the people I encountered on that day.

In the document *Misericordiae Vultus* (The Face of Mercy), Pope Francis invites us to be **"inspiring preachers of Mercy; heralds of the joy of forgiveness, welcoming, loving, and compassionate confessors, who are most especially attentive to the difficult situations of each person."**

As a Divine Word Missionary ministering as a hospital chaplain, I feel blessed to have the opportunity to be a bearer of works of mercy to patients—visiting the sick, comforting the afflicted, counseling the doubtful, and praying for the living and the dead.

As I continue my journey in this ministry, it is my desire to live out the invitation of Pope Francis: **"Once we have received the refreshment and comfort of Christ, we are called in turn to become refreshment and comfort for our brothers and sisters, carried out with a meek and humble attitude, in imitation of the Master."** It is a time for me to become a forgiving minister, to humbly beg for mercy from our loving God and give mercy to others by what I do as a follower of Christ.

-------------------- 📖 --------------------

Words from Saint Arnold Janssen

"Our goal is not to have a life that is free from sorrows, but to bear heavy burdens by the power of the Holy Spirit. Let us, in union with Jesus, endure such burdens to bear fruit of the Kingdom."

For reflection
- In daily life how do I experience God's mercy?
- In what ways am I able to be a bearer of the works of mercy?

Home: Where a missionary's journey begins

In June of 2016, I had the opportunity to spend vacation in my home country, the Philippines. I left the Philippines five years earlier to seek greener pasture in a foreign land and to provide for my family's needs.

Unexpectedly, I ended up joining the Society of the Divine Word's Chicago Province in the United States to pursue religious missionary life. I did not ask my family's approval, but I conscientiously considered them in my serious decision-making.

When considering the religious life, one of my major concerns was the idea of giving up or detaching myself from my family and friends. When I became a Divine Word religious missionary, I struggled with living far from my family, relatives and friends.

There were several times when I missed them terribly. I thought that I had to end my connections or relationships with them to focus more on my desire to serve other people in my ministry. I was wrong.

I learned that my relationships with family and friends change, but they never end. The Divine Word community recognizes and values the vital role and presence of our families as well as our friends not only in our formation but also throughout our religious missionary life.

As a matter of fact, each confrere in our community has the privilege of taking a home leave in his home country once during the years of formation in temporary vows. Every member is given the home leave opportunity to develop healthy and lasting relationships with his loved ones.

Personally, my experience of homecoming was very special, profound and meaningful. I experienced once again the life-giving presence of God, who continuously affirms and deepens my vocation.

During my vacation, I had the opportunity to attend and enjoy several reunions with old friends from my childhood years, classmates in high school and college, former colleagues during my teaching years, fellow Church ministers, mentors, professors and other significant people who have been part of my journey.

I met with my best friend and a few close friends who have been supporting and guiding me in all of my life's endeavors. I was delighted to be with them as we recalled and reminisced about the memorable moments that we had in the past: joys, sadness, failures, misunderstandings, conflicts, adventures, mistakes, arguments and growth.

I was amazed how our paths had crossed at one point in our lives. Each of them made a unique and transforming impact on my life journey. They are people in my life who are not merely friends whom I "like" and "follow" on Facebook, Instagram and Twitter. They are friends whom God sent to me so that I can offer them my physical presence and let them receive my comments filled with love.

These relationships reaffirm my belief that God sends the people I need at the right times, occasions and circumstances. Through them, God teaches me various ways of building and establishing relationships that are integral and essential in accomplishing the ministry entrusted to me as a religious missionary.

One more thing I enjoyed much during my vacation was revisiting the beautiful and significant places that gave me memories and life lessons. These places reflect my life's crossroads where I had relevant turning points in the past. I went back to my former schools where I studied and earned my degrees. I went to my former workplaces where I, as a teacher, urged my students to make a change in society.

I visited several gardens, theme parks, malls and other places where I spent my childhood and teenage years. I attended Masses at parishes where I discovered my passion for serving God in the parish. I also made a pilgrimage to churches that have spiritual significance in my vocation discernment.

Going back to these places led me to realize that change is a relentless reality. The unending change in the physical surrounding in those places is the manifestation of continuous progress and development. It's part of the progress of humanity.

In continuous change, God shows his unceasing initiative of making every individual a better person. I realize that those places serve as avenues for me to discover my own strengths and overcome my weaknesses, taking every opportunity that comes my way and risking the obstacles to overcome my limitations.

More importantly, I have developed and strengthened my desire to seek and trust God in places where I go. As advised by an elder Divine Word priest: in faith, God will always bring us to a place where the divine will of God will unfold. My visit to those places has led me to recall and realize the spiritual encounters I had with God in the past.

Words from Saint Arnold Janssen

"When things go against us, remember that God the Lord in His great wisdom and love still guides and directs us. We can trust and have patience because God will bring good out of whatever happens."

For reflection
- Who are the influences in my life that help me become more aware of God's call?
- What were the significant places and memorable experiences that led me to a deeper and closer encounter with God?

Home: Renewing family relationships

My home leave would not be complete or as meaningful without spending quality time with my beloved family. I celebrated my first anniversary in religious vows with them. I enjoyed every minute that I spent with them. I felt great longing to catch up with them to fill up the five, long years we missed spending together, especially with my siblings. I had so much fun with my grown-up nieces and nephews. I now have a stronger admiration for my mom and stepfather who have persevered in their commitment of loving each other despite many challenges in their relationship.

I came to a deeper realization that, though I did not have the chance to choose the perfect family, I have many choices and chances to help my own family become a God-given blessing in my life.

All the learning experiences I gained while growing up with my family, such as values, behaviors, attitudes and abilities, have become gifts that I share with other families whom I serve in my ministry. My home leave gave me the chance to restore and renew my relationship with my family.

Coming home also was a completion of one of my missions in life—to meet and get to know my long lost biological father. T.S. Eliot once wrote that "we shall not cease from exploration, and the end of all our exploring will be to arrive where we started and know the place for the first time."

Finally, after more than 30 years of longing to know my father, my searching has come to an end. It was the hardest event during my vacation. Honestly, I have wished that the first and only time I met my father could have been just a simple and ordinary event. But, for me—someone who had been through a lot of pain and sufferings in life—it was not easy to face a person who made a decision in the past that I thought caused my life to be different and difficult.

Reconnecting with my father was emotionally challenging. Thanks to a good friend who accompanied and supported me in doing this life-changing encounter with my estranged father, I deeply and strongly believe that my meeting with my father was a particular grace.

It was a grace-filled moment of healing, forgiveness and reconciliation. I do still have unanswered questions, but I don't have to rush to address those concerns. For it is true indeed that God will always answer our prayers according to his divine time and plan.

Meeting my father was a concrete experience of finding and retrieving the missing piece of my being. It was a spiritual experience of rediscovering my self-identity and reaffirming my faith that God, the merciful and loving Father, called me to serve others.

My home visit fulfilled my expectations and hopes. They are all now a part of my joyful memories and meaningful life experiences, not just hoped for events about which I worry. It was such a God-given gift to spend vacation with many wonderful people. They have moved on with their lives, but I am grateful for being able to reconnect with them in ways that were very meaningful for me, ways that I needed to experience with them personally.

The two-and-a-half month vacation in my homeland was a break from my formation. I am deeply joyful and grateful that I had opportunities to be reunited with people who have been part of my vocation; be blessed with learning experiences through visits to significant places in my life; be renewed and restored in my relationships with my family; and be rediscovered in my identity and rejuvenated in my vocation as a Divine Word Missionary.

    I was sad to again leave my home, especially my family. I feel what Jesus felt in Luke 4:38-44 when people sought him and would have kept him from leaving them. My heart urges me that I "must preach the Good News of the Kingdom of God to the other cities also; for I was sent for this purpose."

    I carry with me the joy, gratitude and hope that my home leave has given to me—the essentials that I need to fulfill my God-given mission. Home is where my missionary journey begins.

-------------------- 📖 --------------------

Words from Saint Arnold Janssen

"Happy are those who do not shrink at leaving their homeland, leaving their own people, taking up a life of a thousand sacrifices and privations in order to win people for Christ."

For reflection

- How's my relationship with my family?
- Is there a need for healing, forgiveness, and reconciliation?
- How do I see the role of my family in my vocation?

Trees planted by streams: Seeing God's grace in the arbor

On a cold morning while waiting at the bus stop, I noticed something different about the trees that line the sidewalks. The columns of trees were like knights with swords raised, giving honor. The colorful leaves on the trees that I enjoyed were gone.

Then I recalled seeing three men on a truck. They cut the branches and removed the leaves from the trees a few days ago. I realized winter was coming. As part of preparation for the change of seasons, people in this part of western Spain cut tree branches.

Instead of letting the dry leaves fall to the ground by themselves, they cut the branches to avoid spending time and energy cleaning the fallen, dried leaves from the street.

I wondered if those trees have feelings. What would the trees be feeling with their bare branches and trunks, absent of their colorful and beautiful leaves? I wondered how they would feel knowing that, as the new season approaches, their branches would be cut to spare their owners the inconvenience of raking dried leaves. Would the trees feel that they were sacrificing their possessions for the sake of convenience?

The trees now are completely bare. They have lost their beauty. The rough surfaces and scars of their trunks are more visible—ugly in the eyes of many people. Perhaps they experience pain without the leaves that protect their trunks from the heat of the direct sunlight.

It is as if they are incomplete, imperfect, and weak, standing along the side streets. These feelings lingered inside of me as I passed the trees along the street.

On another morning, I noticed something about the appearance of the bare trees that amused me. Each tree still had at least one branch that touched the branch of another tree. The columns of trees on each side of the street were connected to each other.

It looked like the trees were holding hands, standing and giving support to each other. This stirring image of the bare trees helped transform my feelings of incompleteness, imperfections, and weakness into joy, love, and hope. It gave me peace when I realized that in times when the trees were seemingly vulnerable in their stripped condition, they had each other. With their branches connected, they backed and supported each other.

We, too, experience nakedness and aloneness. There are moments in our lives when we realize our incompleteness, imperfections, and inner and hidden insecurities.

Those insecurities and uncertainties come in many forms. Some people are enslaved by their shamefulness of being part of a broken and dysfunctional family. There are a significant number of individuals who are afraid to admit and address their addictions to drugs, pornography, computer gaming, alcohol, etc. Some friends and co-workers fret about living as undocumented immigrants in our society.

We have abusive political authorities who exteriorly show a powerful stance but interiorly feel guilt for their unjust and oppressive leadership. In a multitude of ways, we hurt from the pain of racial and gender discrimination. Fear, judgment, criticism, condemnation, rejection, isolation, abandonment, and hopelessness—these strong and damaging realities can make people wicked, wounded, broken, weak, and impoverished as individuals and as a community.

Like the bare trees that appear ugly and unattractive, we are vulnerable. That vulnerability sometimes makes us uncomfortable, troubled, ashamed or afraid. Our vulnerabilities sometimes urge us to isolate ourselves from others.

Yet, facing our vulnerabilities is an opportunity to take the path of change—life transformation and conversion. As we gradually grow in relationship with God, we discover his revelation. We come to know his unconditional mercy that can only be experienced by having a deep and intimate relationship with him. In the darkest and ugliest state of our nakedness, we see that sacred mercy and loving embrace of God. We realize that we are not alone. We feel that we do not have to face our vulnerabilities alone.

There is more to learn from those bare trees. Psalms 1:1-3 reads, "Blessed is the man who does not walk in the counsel of the wicked, nor stand in the way of sinners, nor sit in company with scoffers. Rather, the law of the Lord is his joy; and on his law he meditates day and night. He is like a tree planted near streams of water, that yields its fruit in season; its leaves never wither; whatever he does prospers."

The bare trees, as one of God's creations, depend on the grace of their Creator. So do we. It is only through our God's mercy that we are rescued from the power of darkness and brought into a life of freedom. As we continue to witness the greatness of the seasonal change around us, let us bring into our prayers our desire to seek God's mercy.

------------------- 📖 -------------------
Words from Saint Arnold Janssen

"We ought to remember that everything contrary to our will can be a fine opportunity for our growth in perfection. Therefore, we do not turn a deaf ear and do not think that our opponents are all wrong, but think about ourselves and whether we can use this as an opportunity to improve ourselves."

For reflection
- What are my God-given gifts?
- How much aware am I of my weaknesses and insecurities, particularly my traits and characteristics that make me vulnerable?
- What do I find most helpful in sustaining my faith that God accepts and loves me for who I am?

Social challenge: The gifts and tasks of learning a language

What is language? Is there an ultimate language that could transform our world into a better place? I have listened to many speeches on social media from passionate individuals who invite, inspire, and challenge people around the world to make a difference.

Despite the great words, there are still people who are suffering from hunger, war, poverty, violence, discrimination, injustice and other social ills. This thought came to mind during a moment of exhaustion and exasperation during my Spanish-language studies.

When I came to Spain for my two-year cross-cultural training program, I was filled with inspiration, hope and excitement for living in a foreign land as a religious missionary.

Similar to my move to the United States years ago, I have carried with me an open mind and a willing heart. I looked forward to learning a new language and culture. However, I started feeling exasperated after a few months of language studies. I have difficulty learning the verbs and their conjugated forms and tenses. I also struggle with the proper use of masculine or feminine articles and determining whether a noun is singular or plural.

Despite the support of my community, the language barrier made me feel isolated. I even began to lose enthusiasm for attending daily Mass. I felt as though I was only physically present. I did not like reading the missalette and being unable to understand the text. I was stressed and disconnected from the spirit of the Eucharistic celebration. This experience led me to question my vocation as a religious missionary.

Several times, I asked myself, "Why am I learning another language?" I thought it would be fun and exciting, but I have come to realize the enormous difficulties and challenges entailed in learning a new language. I questioned God, "Why is learning Spanish so difficult?" When I become frustrated with all the mistakes I make while practicing Spanish, I go to our chapel and vent all my complaints and frustration in prayer.

It is worth waiting for God's response. As time passes, I see God's marvelous way of enlightening my mind, purifying my heart and directing my will toward my language study. I learned profound lessons.

Language gives us the power to free those who are oppressed in our society. I have met several migrants who have had difficulty conversing in Spanish because they did not have the means to learn the language in a formal school. Most of them are self-taught through their daily interactions in their jobs, and some of their employers take advantage of their limitations.

Language is dynamic and transformative. One of my difficulties with Spanish is knowing the right context to use certain verbs. An English verb can have multiple translations in Spanish, and each translation has a different meaning. Thus, it is important to know the right word, understand its right context, and use it appropriately.

I am aware that no words can sufficiently describe the suffering that refugees endure, but I want my mind and heart to be transformed by the words they utter.

I was intrigued to learn that in Spanish, verbs not only describe action, they also express feelings embedded in each word. My eagerness to learn Spanish verbs has led me to a greater desire to deeply understand the words I hear from suffering refugees.

Living in Europe has made me more aware of the refugee crisis. Many refugees were forced to flee their home countries because of persecution, war or violence. Now as they try to start a new life in Europe, they struggle with racial discrimination, religious persecution, political intimidation, harassment and death threats.

My discomfort with communicating in Spain is nothing compared to the hardships that refugees face, especially with their struggles to learn the language. I am aware that no words can sufficiently describe the suffering that refugees endure, but I want my mind and heart to be transformed by the words they utter.

Language is a channel for ethical, doctrinal and spiritual understanding that builds a better society. Learning the Spanish language has made me become more aware of the gap between the language of the elders and the language of the youth. Perhaps, the gap has become so wide that we have neglected each other.

It is hard not to feel sad and dismayed whenever I attend the Holy Mass every Sunday in Spain. The physical grandiosity of the church, with its intricate and marvelous designs, cannot hide the truth that it is an almost empty space.

The church is only full of people on two occasions: when there are groups of tourists and during funeral services. Most of the people who attend Sunday Mass are elderly. Just as I lost my enthusiasm for the Mass because I could not understand the language, maybe many youths nowadays do not understand the significance of words about religion and faith.

It is my hope that through the language we speak, we will be able to carry with us the teaching, moral norms and values embedded in the words. There is an invitation for all of us to revive the language of values that can greatly contribute to the transformation of our community.

What is the ultimate language that could transform our world into a better place? I honestly do not have an answer.

One might suggest that humility, kindness and charity are the language that will transform us. With perseverance, faith and hope, I am one among many people who are searching for that unifying language.

The word that urges me to continue my journey is "us." Where two or more are gathered, there is the Divine Word that became flesh in our world. Let us transform our society into a better world by living the gifts and tasks of learning a language. And, let us begin with the word "us."

-------------------- 📖 --------------------

Words from Saint Arnold Janssen

"We must be humble also towards ourselves: humble in thinking and desiring, humble in speech, humble in our clothing and in our exterior behavior. We must be humble in dealing with others and despise no one, but meet all with due attention and respect."

For reflection

- What means could I employ to help our society become a better place?
- How can I use these means effectively?

God's peculiar grace

As I lay in my bed late one night, I received an unexpected Facebook message from a good friend. When asked, he told me that he was "a bit tired, a bit perturbed, a bit sad."

His message troubled me, so I stayed up to continue chatting with him. He shared with me how the upcoming Advent and Christmas seasons make him feel sad and angry. His mother's only sibling, his aunt, died on Christmas Day four years ago.

Then two years later, his dear grandmother suffered a car accident. They thought she would survive to be with them for Christmas. Sadly, it wasn't meant to be and his family had to make the difficult decision to remove his grandmother's ventilator on Dec. 24. She passed away on Christmas Eve.

At that moment, I wished I had a thousand words that would bridge the thousands of miles between us. I can't imagine the amount of pain his family feels because of these two losses. I completely understand his saying bluntly that he was angry.

I wished at that moment that I could provide my physical presence. We were on different sides of the world. Whilst he was just beginning the day in the United States, I was ending mine in Spain. I looked out of my bedroom window and saw the shining stars in the night sky.

My friend is like one of the stars that sparkle in the dark sky. In spite of grappling with the emotions in his heart—emotions that make him want to give up—he strives to keep the light of hope. Many people struggle with their anger, resentment and loneliness. They desperately try to nurture a hopeful and joyful spirit and experience the meaning of Advent in their lives.

Social conflicts throughout our world are weakening the spirit of hope among us. Our desire for peace, unity, and love is robbed from us by terrible events everywhere.

In the news, we read about arrogance, hate, racism and discrimination. We see powerful nations tyrannize defenseless ones. We see national leaders who advocate the use of violence to solve their nations' epidemic social ills.

Some nations are closing their borders to victims of injustice, survivors fleeing from wars. Many displaced people are taking risks to find new homes while political leaders debate how to deal with increasing arrivals of refugees and migrants.

Many immigrants died from starvation, sickness and drowning as they traveled the ocean. We see evil in our world. We cry out, asking ourselves how much we truly value human dignity. Chaos enslaves us. We are lost in darkness. We are getting tired of waiting, preparing and hoping for the coming of that day when all suffering will be over.

Yet, the Advent season can be a source of peculiar grace for which each of us longs. Like me, you probably have heard a friend's painful story. The daily news we hear from around the world keeps us informed about the disturbing and heartbreaking anguish of our fellow human beings. The suffering we all experience in various ways connects us to each other.

It urges us to pause and reflect, making us realize that we should not obey the dictates of darkness in society. We all seek for a day when we are filled with faith, hope and love. We wait for that day. We prepare for that day. We hope for that day.

When we live out the spirit of waiting, preparing and hoping for that God-given desire, we recognize and receive the peculiar grace of the Advent season.

It is said that the stars are like beacons of hope for all the lost souls of the world. They enable us to be enlightened if we seek the spark of God's infinite mercy and love.

When embraced in times of sufferings, the love of God keeps us whole. It preserves human dignity when the world tries to mangle it. The season of Advent makes us believe that in the midst of the world's sinfulness—envy, gluttony, greed, lust, pride, sloth and wrath—we can help to restore humanity if we allow the Spirit of the Lord to rest upon us.

When we accept the Lord, we realize that through the Spirit of wisdom and understanding, the Spirit of counsel and strength, the Spirit of knowledge and fear of the Lord, we are able to overcome the trials and hardships before us.

The same Holy Spirit that blessed Mary by calling her to be the bearer of the Savior of the world lets us all welcome God into our lives. By learning from God's words, ways and instructions, we will be transformed. And when we are transformed, we transform our chaotic world into a dwelling place of hope, peace and love. Could all this be possible? Yes! For nothing is impossible for God.

Words from Saint Arnold Janssen

"How important it is to follow the inspiration of grace! For if we have a feeling to do good but do not do it, this grace is lost and also all graces which would follow it. Through the cooperation with grace we obtain new graces; and so grace follows on grace or loss follows on loss.

For reflection
- What are the social concerns that affect me most?
- What are the gifts and tasks that God has given me in order to respond to the needs of my community?

The earthen vessels of Parroquia Nuestra Señora de Altagracia

When I finished my seven months of language study in the Province of Palencia, I moved into a Divine Word community in Madrid. The former formation house is now the residence of the Divine Word chaplains who are ministering to various migrant communities, including immigrants from Africa, Poland, China and the Philippines. I had the privilege of doing pastoral ministry at Parroquia Nuestra Señora de Altagracia. It is geographically located in Valdezarza, a neighborhood in Madrid. The congregation is made up of people from Mexico, Peru, India, Togo, Philippines and Spain.

A small but vibrant community

The church is small, simple and ordinary compared to some of the more famous Spanish churches. One might not recognize the building as a church if not for the bell tower and the signage. However, there is more to the parish than the church's simple facade.

Parishes in Spain face two challenges: a decrease in volunteers and a scarcity of youth in parish communities. Most of the parishioners who participate regularly at Altagracia are elders. They recognized the situation with sadness and frustration. But rather than give up on the parish community, they respond to the challenge with courage and hope.

With the help of the two Divine Word priests, they make the most out of what they have: time and presence. The parish community of Altagracia lives out what it means to be a church today. They respond to the call for inclusion, dialogue and faith encounter.

Some of the elders are isolated in our society because of failing health. Others are widowed, physically handicapped or sick. They come to the parish daily for the Holy Mass even though their physical limitations make it difficult. They offer their struggles as their sacrifice to God.

The parish addresses their psychological, emotional, social and spiritual needs. In return, their presence animates the life and work of the parish. Not only do they attend the liturgical celebration; depending upon their capabilities, they also volunteer.

The elders are very passionate storytellers. Their stories give everyone a sense of belonging, acceptance and love. Indeed, parish community is a living testimony that all are welcome in our Church.

Prophetic Dialogue

Altagracia parishioners have a passion for dialogue. They are diverse and are varied ages, ethnicities, cultures, social statuses and political affiliations. The liturgy is the center and common ground for everyone.

Dialogue is apparent in their various parish activities, such as the Vida Ascendiente, a weekly faith group sharing of the elders; the catechesis of children preparing for First Communion and Confirmation; and the Bible study group. Moreover, the dialogue in the parish community is animated and strengthened through special occasions, such as the profession of religious vows, ordinations, birthdays and anniversaries. In these encounters, the parish community experiences personal and communal transformation, which comes through listening, questioning and sharing.

The elders have time and presence that they share as gifts out of love to others. They are like the poor widow who offered her two copper coins as tithes in the treasury. Jesus praised her for giving the smallest of coins in contrast with the rich who gave greater sums (Luke 21:1-4).

It gives them deep joy from selfless giving and generous love for others in the community. In the spirit of generosity and sacrifice, they praise God saying, "God Himself gives to us that we may give in turn." Undeniably, their volunteerism reflects their authentic faith encounter with God.

God's earthen vessels

The elders at Altagracia are like earthen vessels, pots made of clay. The parish community consists of precious earthen vessels created to be receptacles for its intended contents – inclusion, dialogue and faith.

This parish may not look like a grand museum and may not be filled with tourists, but it strongly embodies the Church that quenches our thirst for God's blessings. God's blessings pour upon us when the parish community is present—believing, praying and loving.

I admired how a community in a simple and ordinary parish could make a difference in making our society a better place. If you have a chance, I encourage you to visit and receive the graces of Parroquia Nuestra Señora de Altagracia.

Words from Saint Arnold Janssen

"**Kindness and gentleness never come alone. They presuppose many other virtues and a heart filled with love.**"

For reflection
- Do I recognize the role of my relationship with my parish community in discovering my vocation?
- What are the common and relevant values in my parish that help me grow as a person?

The quest and the questions

El Camino de Santiago is one of the world's oldest pilgrimage routes, a journey across Northern Spain toward the Cathedral of Santiago in Galicia, where pilgrims can view and venerate the apostle's tomb.

Like many pilgrims, I entered into the Camino in hopes that the walk would deepen my spiritual growth and transform my life. Along the way, I also met cyclists and hikers who were simply seeking an adventure.

Some individuals journeyed alone while others preferred to journey with a group. I walked with a youth group called Verbo Joven from one of our Divine Word parishes. The group consisted of 26 individuals—18 teenagers, four parents, two priests and two seminarians. While we hiked as one community with a shared goal, each of us had a different and significant reason for partaking in the Camino de Santiago.

The week before I left for the Camino, a confrere visited me in Madrid. As we caught up on each other's lives, he repeated the following phrase several times: "My brother, do not lose Him." His message baffled me as I prepared to leave for the trip. As I pondered his words, more questions began to emerge in my mind: "My God, am I losing You in my life?" "Am I walking away from You?" "Am I happy with the level and quality of my relationship with You, my Lord?"

At that point, I could not answer those questions with any certainty. I happened to begin the Camino on the second anniversary of a special occasion in my life—my profession of vows as a Divine Word Missionary.

I looked back and reflected on the many things that have transpired during the past few years. The Camino signs along the path, showing the distance to Santiago, reminded me of the many crossroads in my vocation journey.

Thinking about my life in Spain—learning another foreign language, adapting to the lifestyle and culture, and understanding the faith life of the people—has helped me become more conscious of my discernment of the religious missionary life and whether it is truly the life that I want to live.

Questions are a natural part of life. During the Camino pilgrimage, each time I saw a sign indicating the distance to the destination, I asked, "How many kilometers left?" I kept asking the same question again and again. I realized that every time I asked the question, I received a different answer. Whenever I saw the sign with the distance, I knew that I was getting closer to my destination.

In Christian life, we also have lots of questions, particularly about the quality of our lives and how we see God's role and involvement in our lives. Sadly, many of us who have confusing and troubling questions might become weak in our faith in God.

The Camino gave me precious time for meditation. Where do we come from? Where are we going? What must we do? I thought of so many life questions that lead me closer to God. When we are overwhelmed with life's questions, let us be still. God is there waiting for us to be open to His great revelation.

-------------------- 📖 --------------------

Words from Saint Arnold Janssen

"Through meditation our inner life will be made perfect. This is very hard work and is a task for our whole life. Therefore, let us strive after it unflinchingly through cooperation with divine grace to reach perfection."

For reflection
- What is my image of God?
- How does it help me grow in my faith life?
- What are some questions in life that I would like to ask God about?

The backpack

The Camino may not be easy and fun for those who hate walking long distances while carrying a heavy backpack. I can imagine the suffering of those who are impatient when dealing with unexpected and inconvenient situations. These matters are not a bother, though, for pilgrims who long for a Camino experience that is one-of-a-kind, special and indelible on one's heart.

A meaningful Camino is attainable when a pilgrim pays attention to his or her surroundings, such as signs, people, feelings, thoughts, desires, intuitions, desires and encounters along the way.

My backpack made all the difference in my Camino experience. I was grateful that a friend lent his durable backpack to me. I intentionally brought only basic and essential items: a fleece jacket, hat, toiletries, towel, raincoat, flashlight, sleeping bag, a pair of dry-fit shirts, shorts, socks and undergarments. I did not want my back and shoulders to suffer from the heavy load.

Other pilgrims possessed a variety of backpacks. They carried backpacks that varied in color, size, shapes and brands. Seeing the pilgrims walking in front me with their different and colorful backpack was like watching butterflies. Some backpacks were filled with only important content to help them survive the journey.

Pilgrims often consider their backpacks their best companion because it is with them most of the time. There were, however, some pilgrims who suffered and complained about their bags. There were those who did not properly pack. Along the way, I saw personal items, such as shoes, shirts and sleeping bags, lying on the side of the road.

To me, the backpacks depicted the burdens of life. They represented health issues, family problems, financial responsibilities, relationship conflicts, job concerns, identity crises, and the list goes on. Each of us has concerns, burdens and challenges in our daily lives. Like the pilgrims' backpacks, we carry the burdens of life on our shoulders. Most of us have experienced that point where we feel that the burden is too cumbersome and we can no longer bear it.

There were some groups that traveled without a backpack. They hired a carrier service to transfer their backpack to the next destination and freed themselves from the burden of carrying a heavy backpack during the walk. Some might say that the ability to carry a loaded backpack on our shoulders shapes and molds a person into a true pilgrim. Others might say that each of us must learn to understand our own limitations.

We need someone, such as our family, relatives and friends, not necessarily to carry our burdens but to assist us. Above all, we must humble ourselves to embrace the truth that we need God in our lives.

-------------------- 📖 --------------------

Words from Saint Arnold Janssen
"We are on earth to grow in virtue and to live with holy trust in God, enduring patiently all sorrows and sufferings."

For reflection
- How do I cope with burdens in my life?
- Do I have a support group whom I depend on?
- How do I grow in virtue and strengthen my faith in God?

A journey through nature

Being an early riser gave me an advantage when I traveled as a pilgrim on the Camino de Santiago in Northern Spain. I am one who habitually wakes up early in the day and feels energetic.

On the pilgrimage, many seekers woke up early to begin walking before sunrise. On several consecutive mornings, our group began walking in the darkness of the cold morning. In predawn, we could not see our surrounding. I followed our lead, who carried a flashlight as a guide. I was scared walking alone in the dark.

I maintained a close proximity to my companion so I would not get lost in the middle of the forest. At one point, I did not notice that my group was far ahead of me. I missed the sign and lost the right path. I'm grateful to my fellow pilgrim who came back to find me. I did not want to be alone in darkness.

What I enjoyed most about beginning our walk early in the morning was the chance to witness the amazing first light in the sky before sunrise. I fell in love with the marvelous scenery as the sunlight gradually filled the sky. The horizon dramatically unfolded its beauty before my eyes. It seemed like the fields, mountain, trees and animals rejoiced with the pilgrims. What a wonderful mystery nature is! The dynamics of nature teach us to journey out of darkness towards the light.

Some pilgrims came to the Camino with a weak faith. They were longing for God's companionship and seeking direction in their faith life. One afternoon while attending Mass in a parish church, I was moved by a woman who began weeping upon hearing the Scripture reading. The tears that flowed down the woman's face the moment she heard the Word of God reminded me how the sacred Scriptures serve as a guiding light and the comforting presence of God during dark moments. During the Camino, pilgrims give themselves a chance to acknowledge and allow God to be more closely present to them.

-------------------- 📖 --------------------

Words from Saint Arnold Janssen

"We know that we cannot solve all problems with the strength we now possess, but we hope that the dear God will grant us all that is necessary for us to do so. For we know God is there, and we always know where we can find God, where God allows Himself to be found and is waiting for us."

For reflection

- What is a natural phenomenon that causes me to feel awe and wonder?
- What is the life lesson that God teaches me through nature?

'Buen camino!' A greeting of connection and friendship

Considering the madness in our world, it is not surprising that many pilgrims take part in the Camino, seeking spiritual enlightenment. The firsthand testimonies that I heard from fellow pilgrims, as well as the stories that I read on blogs about the Camino experience, made me believe more deeply that the pilgrim's desire is to grow in the grace and knowledge of God.

To attain such an experience, one has to slow down and be patient. The Camino de Santiago is not a speed race that forces one to walk rapidly. It is not a long-distance tournament that makes one greater than the person who took longer to walk the path. While pace and rhythm are two important aspects of the Camino pilgrimage, what matters most is reaching the destination with memorable and meaningful encounters with others along the path.

The Camino gave me time to detach and disconnect from the busyness of the world. I intentionally avoided getting information about the things happening in the world and contacted only a few individuals while on the journey. It was a struggle not to look at social media during the journey. There were many times when I was tempted to post photos of the beautiful scenery. However, I wanted to give myself the opportunity to look internally and be with God. Ironically, the more I detached and disconnected myself from people, the more I felt their closeness and connection.

My family, close friends, Divine Word community, mentors and other significant people filled my mind and heart. I spent time remembering and understanding the meaning and purpose of their presence in my life. Through God's grace, I once again reassessed the level and quality of my relationships with the people in my life and how I meaningfully partake in growing, maturing, deepening my relationships and understanding my communion with significant people in my life.

Along the Camino journey, pilgrims greeted one another with the phrase *"buen camino,"* which literally means "good path." It's generally understood as "good luck and happy traveling." Camino pilgrims come from different places, backgrounds, ethnicities, languages and cultures. The exchange of the greeting *buen camino* is a concrete act of recognizing and sharing presence with fellow pilgrims.

It may be taken as a simple gesture of greeting another person, but it also could lead to a new and deep connection. It's the first step toward friendship where two or more people open themselves and become their best selves. The greeting, when extended from the heart, could be followed by one's sharing of identity, relationship, purpose and meaning in life.

My interactions and conversations with fellow pilgrims have reminded me that each of us has crossroads in our lives. Sometimes, we share the same journey. Sometimes, we journey alone. There are times when we voyage as strangers with other strangers. The one thing we all have in common is our longing to make our journey a meaningful one. We are invited to open our eyes to the presence of others and their needs. Let it be a source of joy in our mission. *Buen camino!*

Words from Saint Arnold Janssen

"It is good to do something that we know is pleasant for our neighbor, i.e., to say a friendly word. Then all goes better. Let us perform deeds of loving service for one another."

For reflection

- What personal characteristics or traits do I possess that give joy to others?
- Do I invest the necessary time and effort in building and keeping friendships?
- How do I nurture my relationship with the people I meet in my faith journey?

The end and beginning of the grace-filled journey

One of the many highlights of the pilgrimage was our last stop before reaching the cathedral: Monte de Gozo (Mount of Joy). Located on the top of a hill, Monte de Gozo offers great views of the city and the tower of the Cathedral of Santiago de Compostela.

The scenery gave us a glimpse of what lay ahead and motivated us to finish our journey. As the end of our journey came into view, we began to share our joy, gratitude and hope with one another. Indeed, happiness is real when shared.

Undeniably, the most unforgettable moment during the Camino pilgrimage was our arrival at the Cathedral of Santiago de Compostela. I felt my heart rejoice in the Lord whom I believe accompanied me through the journey.

A special Bible passage came to mind, "I have competed well; I have finished the race; I have kept the faith." (2 Timothy 4:7). I remembered and felt the words of Saint Paul who may have known Saint James. Upon our arrival, my companions and I were not able to contain our inner joy. Our eyes were filled with tears as we embraced one another in appreciation.

Other pilgrims who arrived after us shouted, chanted and danced out of happiness and gratitude. We could not believe that we had arrived. Unfortunately, we were unable to attend the Pilgrims' Mass because when we arrived the cathedral was at maximum capacity. So we waited in the winding line outside where other pilgrims talked and took pictures.

After Mass, we entered the cathedral. I felt its sacred ambiance. I venerated Saint James's tomb, located under the altar, and presented my physical and spiritual tiredness in front of the grave. I prayed that the Lord might accept all the hardships and sacrifices endured during the pilgrimage and that they may give greater glory to God.

I then went above the altar to embrace the statue of Saint James as a symbolic gesture of my petition to God—that through the intercession of Saint James, God will embrace my family, relatives, friends, loved ones and everyone for whom I promised to pray. May God take away their sufferings and bless them with joy, love, peace and hope.

I was struck by the on-going construction inside and outside the cathedral—like a metaphor or invitation for all the pilgrims on the Camino. Like the cathedral under construction, each pilgrim is called to conversion.

Each person has his or her imperfections, weaknesses and rough edges. But when feelings of brokenness are acknowledged humbly and accepted wholeheartedly, they can be stepping stones toward life-giving gifts to others. Pilgrims are not called to go to church; we are called to become the living Church of Christ.

With my credential, a Camino passport full of different stamps from places that I passed, I got my Compostela. It is the certification, or diploma, that serves as proof that I completed the Camino de Santiago. For me, the Compostela is not simply about my arrival at the end of the Camino de Santiago. It is a remembrance of the grace-filled spiritual journey that urges me to begin a new life-long pilgrimage.

In the cathedral's Chapel of Saint Mark, I found a pilgrim reflection guide. It offered meaningful insights and questions that helped me contemplate my experience. I read words that touched me deeply: "To arrive in Santiago is not the end of our Camino. In a way, it is a place of departure. On the Camino de Santiago, as well as in life, the goals impel us to new horizons."

Enlightened by the wisdom of the Holy Spirit, I believe that my arrival at the Cathedral of Saint James urges me to do something more in my life journey. I accept the invitation that I read in the pilgrim reflection guide: "To arrive…To arrive is not to finish the path you began. To arrive is to want to carry on from the path you have walked. To arrive is to glimpse a future horizon which was nourished in the meetings and challenges along the way. To arrive is to announce that a new way of looking is present in daily life. To arrive is to perceive that everything remains the same, but you are not as you were at the beginning. To arrive is to have the wisdom to start walking again to the place this same path guides you." My whole Camino experience has deepened and strengthened my prayer to God.

-------------------- 📖 --------------------

Words from Saint Arnold Janssen

"The true way to happiness is the fulfillment of God's divine Will. Whoever seeks his happiness along another path, will find thorns and thistles already here on earth and earn a deserved push."

For reflection

- How do I feel in the midst of the crisis that our Church is dealing with?
- Have I thought of leaving the Church?
- What are the concrete actions that I would like to do for the people of God?

An Emmaus journey in Niebla

At the end of Easter Sunday Mass, the presider invited the congregation to sit for a moment. I nervously approached the lectern. I felt every heartbeat in my chest. I was about to bid farewell to the community of Niebla.

As I began to speak, a sudden silence filled the church, and I noticed the eyes of friends fill with tears. I had lived in the village for only six months. It was a short stay, but I've learned a lot. Life in this town is simple and quiet, a departure for me. Having grown up and studied in large cities, I am accustomed to places where people are especially busy with their own affairs. As I leave Niebla, I want to share lessons that the Iliplenses (villagers of Niebla) taught me. I carry them in my heart.

Spend time and share presence with others through a family meal.

I can't remember exactly how many generous invitations I received, but the Iliplenses showed me why the region was named Spain's Gastronomic Capital of 2017. They served local delicacies—white prawns, coquina clams, monkfish, sea bass and cuttlefish; strawberries, raspberries, oranges and asparagus, taken from fertile soil of the area; and *jamon*, Iberian ham, from the mountainous regions of the province. They whet the appetite with white wines, quality liqueurs, grape juice, vinegars and olive oils. I admire their spontaneity and appreciate the honor of spending time with their families. They let me know that they care about me and value my presence in their community.

Greet each other and share smiles with each other.
"¡Hola!, ¿Que tal?, ¿Como va?, Hasta luego!" Members of Las Raíces, an organization of retired people, were good companions. They made a point to ask how I was doing and if I was enjoying life in the village. As someone who lived most of his life in a big city, greeting other people, especially strangers, is not a common practice. This simple gesture made me feel connected and valued by others. It reminded me that we are one loving and thoughtful community.

Fulfill one's duty and responsibility in the family and the community.
Workers in Niebla are dedicated. In a small village like Niebla, it is possible to get to know the people working at the market, grocery store, municipal hall, restaurants and hardware store. In the community, each person fulfills their duty as a service to the community and the family. Each person's vocation serves as a humble contribution to make our world a better place.

Tell and retell life stories and community narratives.
Niebla is a village filled with stories. Every place within the village—Castillo de Niebla, Casa de la Cultura, Iglesia de Santa Maria de la Granada and Rio Tinto–has a tale. Through these stories, I learned about the food, history, culture and faith of the people. The homes are filled with family photos. With those pictures, Iliplenses narrate their stories with passion,

enthusiasm and pride. As I listened, I felt the value and importance of the story to the person telling it. I sensed how the story transformed their lives. Our life experiences are a wise teacher.

Keep the cultural heritage and religious traditions dynamically alive.

As a municipality located in Andalusia, Niebla has a unique cultural heritage and religious tradition. During Holy Week, members of three Las Hermandades, or brotherhoods, lead community celebrations. The members of Hermandad de Virgen del Pino, Hermandad del Rocío, and Hermandad de Jesus Nazareno practice and pass on ways of the Catholic Church. Fiestas and other events, organized by the Ayuntamiento de Niebla each month, leave a memorable impression: La Feria Medieval in November, Los Campanilleros in December, La Cabalgata de los Reyes Magos in January and Semana Santa in April. Communal activities, such as musical concerts and community picnics known as El Toston, bring the people together and pass along traditions from one generation to the next.

Spread the joy, love and hope in the community.

The laypeople in Niebla played an important role in their parish. I learned much from the various lay groups. Members of Lectura Creyente deepen their faith by studying the Scriptures each week. Cáritas assists the less fortunate by providing for their basic needs. Volunteers in Catequistas educate the children in the village and prepare them for receiving the Sacraments. The Pastoral de Salud visit the sick and elders in their homes once a month. The Fieles de la Santa Eucaristía attends daily Mass. These groups have fewer numbers than in years past, but they are dedicated in spreading the joy, love and hope of the Risen Christ.

My experience in Niebla was an Emmaus journey. My new friends reminded me how Christians keep faith in the Risen Lord, even amidst scarcity and adversity.

---------------------- 📖 ----------------------
Words from Saint Arnold Janssen
"If we live in community, it is not the extraordinary which is the best, but the daily ordinary things."

For reflection
- How do I value and recognize the unique gifts and talents of people serving in the parish for God and others?
- Do I remain loving and supporting in our parish regardless of the messiness and struggles of my life?

Working with the saints next door

Editorial Verbo Divino (EVD) is a global publishing company and the major communication ministry of the Society of the Divine Word in Spain. Located in a small town called Estella, EVD has been serving the Catholic Church since 1956. It plays an essential role in proclaiming the Word of God.

In addition to publishing Bibles in several languages, EVD produces theological books, magazines, journals and prayer booklets. In this digital age, EVD also creatively ventures into new forms of multimedia to make the Divine Word more accessible to the people of God.

During the last phase of my Cross-Cultural Training Program in Spain, I had the opportunity to see the inner workings of EVD and to work with the lay staff and SVD confreres there.

EVD employees busied themselves: laying out publications, editing, accounting, sales, marketing and shipping. I helped digitalize the *latinoamericá* edition of DOCAT, which is a resource for young people who want to learn the social teachings of the Catholic Church.

My main task involved transferring content from one electronic resource into the mobile application software—a lot of copying and pasting. After finishing DOCAT, I received a new task—adding content to *La Buena Noticia*, EVD's daily Scripture mobile application. More copying and pasting.

While working besides my colleagues in the office, I heard them sharing ideas and plans for other projects. I was filled with pride and thought, "I can do that too!" I wished to be a part of other projects, but I also wanted to joyfully accomplish the task assigned to me.

God responded to my prayer. After closer observation, I saw that there is profound meaning in repetitive tasks. My confreres do repetitive work in our community, such as preparing breakfast, shopping for the needs of community, setting the tables for meals and cleaning after the meals. They mow the lawn and care for the gardens.

As missionaries, they arrange the schedule of Mass presiders; preside at Mass; participate in community prayer; join the weekly Bible sharing; and attend funerals to offer condolences.

Likewise, the lay staff have their own repetitive tasks, such as editing, reviewing, conceptualizing, laying out the publications, packing, billing and delivering the orders. All the staff members perform tasks in collaboration with the whole team.

They performed their jobs every day with dedication. I realized that although my tasks seemed simplistic, they contributed to the overall work. I felt fortunate to be part of the team.

In his third apostolic exhortation entitled *Gaudete et Exsultate*, Pope Francis wrote: "Very often it is a holiness found in our next-door neighbours, those who, living in our midst, reflect God's presence."

My colleagues at EVD and in the Divine Word community are those holy neighbors. The daily collection of repetitive tasks makes a sacred routine. Together, we proclaim the Divine Word.

Words from Saint Arnold Janssen

"We should have a joyful, thankful heart and make our gratitude shine through joy each day. We should be joyful at heart and not feel sorrowful remorse. If we sing songs and psalms, it should be done with a joyful heart. Our joyfulness should also show in our dealings with others."

For reflection
- Who are the people in my life that I consider 'saints-next-door'?
- How do I express my joy and gratitude to the people around me?

Christ's compassionate heart

One afternoon while I was running alone on Chicago's lakefront trail, I encountered three teenagers. They looked at me and shouted something. When I removed my earphones to understand what they were saying, I realized that they were cursing me.

One guy gestured obscenely, approached me and hit the back of my head. I thought of fighting back, but I followed my instinct to run away. No one else was nearby, and I thought that they might be carrying a weapon. When I was far away from them and felt safe, I called 911.

After a few minutes, I saw a police car moving towards the teenagers. While I did not have a serious injury, I was worried that the teenagers might do harm to others along the lakeshore.

That evening I had difficulty sleeping. My memory of the incident bothered me. I was filled me with mixed emotions: fear, anger, vengeance, distress. Why did the teenagers harass me? What motivated them to harm strangers?

Such an experience can take away our capacity to be compassionate. When others harm us, it's a challenge to be merciful toward them. I did not take the chance to know personally those teenagers who harassed me, but they may have been raised in their family with a lack of values. They might have grown up without parents or guardians who could teach them to show respect and kindness to neighbors. Perhaps, they were upset with the kind of life they had due to financial, emotional or psychological family conditions.

As Christians, our response should be one of compassion for all who are suffering. We are called to acknowledge their agony and pain. It requires us to be courageous for those who are afraid, strong for those who are weak, generous for those who are deprived, prudent for those who are confused and hopeful for those who are in despair.

Compassion is an intrinsic aspect of human nature. The word compassion is derived from the Latin words *pati* and *cum* which mean "to suffer with."

Compassion is not sentimentality when we see an act of kindness in online viral video, clicking "likes" and emoji reactions. Posting comments on social media cannot genuinely and whole-heartedly express compassion. We must live out compassion through direct human connections, not virtual connections.

Our society needs compassion that calls for justice and forgiveness. All three are necessary in the process of bringing about reconciliation. Domestic violence, gun violence, mental illness, racism and poverty cause wounds of division that call for healing and reconciliation. If we strive for compassion with strong conviction informed by our Christian faith, it can lead us to realize that we can be greater than the society we have now.

The two founders of my religious-missionary congregation, the Society of the Divine Word, taught me what it means to be compassionate to others. Saint Arnold Janssen taught us to serve others so that the heart of Jesus would live in our hearts and the hearts of all. Likewise, Saint Joseph

Freinademetz taught us that, in relating with different people, the only language that is understood by people everywhere is the language of love.

They were impelled by Christ's compassion to serve their neighbors in mission. The heart of Jesus is filled with compassion. It is the love of Christ that enables us to be compassionate with others. As disciples, we are also tasked to clothe ourselves with compassion by doing what Christ did (Colossians 3:12).

We have to let Christ live and remain in us. As St. Paul says, "I live now not with my own life but with the life of Christ who lives in me" (Galatians 2:20). Like Christ, we carry out our vocation as disciples by accompanying those who are in misery, feeling lonely or are mourning. Let us not allow self-centered prejudice to remain in our hearts.

During a weekly general audience in Rome, Pope Francis said that Jesus' compassion toward people in need is not a vague sentiment. Rather, it is a calling for Christians to bring compassion to others. He urged each one of us to share in Christ's compassion.

As human beings created in the image and likeness of God, we are compelled by Jesus to serve others with the compassion of Jesus. Let us ignite compassion in our hearts as our concrete act of solidarity with others that will help eradicate social conflicts and heal the wounds in our relationships. Let us allow Christ to be the focus and guide in our path toward compassionate living.

Words from Saint Arnold Janssen

"Everything human is weighed down with imperfections, behind and in front, right and left. So do not lose your courage if you see such things attached to humanity."

For reflection
- What are the situations that challenge me to become more compassionate?
- Have I joined a socio-religious movement or non-government agency that promotes and upholds social justice?

Faithful friends: Rooted in Jesus

Friendship is a fundamental and essential aspect of any human relationship. I can't imagine a life without friends. They help to make our lives happy and meaningful. While it is easy for me to get along with people, I do not develop friendships quickly. It takes time for me to trust and allow a stranger to become part of my life.

Many people use social media as a channel to build and develop relationships. Some people use Twitter, Facebook, WhatsApp, Skype, Instagram and LinkedIn to keep in touch with their friends. I am sometimes saddened when I see friends engage in arguments on social media. One cannot deny that a large quantity of friends online does not guarantee that a person has true friendships.

Some people consider social networks as a testing ground for true friendship. Many individuals who build online friendships echo the view of *CommsBreakdown* blogger Steve Ash, who believes that "far from making us less sociable, the online world is actually creating an ability to connect and engage with the rest of the world that's never existed in any previous century. It's more than possible for a person to have a network of friends that's truly global, breaking down geographical, cultural and social barriers to build friendships across the planet."

On the other hand, online friendship cannot replace the genuine intimacy of real friendship. I have a small circle of *faithful* friends. Each has a unique and valuable quality that people desire in friends. The qualities of faithful friends described in Sirach 6:14-16 depict the individuals who comprise my circle of friends. As the Scriptures say, "Faithful friends are beyond price, no amount can balance their worth."

Faithful friends are like sturdy shelter. They are like strong pillars that we hold onto when we feel helpless and alone. They welcome and comfort us during times when we face life storms. Faithful friends provide spiritual sanctuary when we experience misery and sorrow. They are reflections of Christ's love, his gentle and consoling presence in our lives. I recognize Christ's protection through faithful friends who stand at my side in difficult times.

Faithful friends are treasures. They are priceless. Together, we enrich our friendships by discovering and sharing our gifts and talents with each other. Faithful friends are not perfect. Like us, they have their imperfections. We accept them for who they are, the way God wants them to be. These friendships are paths that lead us toward closeness with Christ. Christ provides the missing pieces that we and our faithful friends cannot give to each other in friendship.

Jesus is our greatest friend. He is the model and guide of how to be a faithful friend to others of different languages, cultures and beliefs.

Faithful friends are a life-saving remedy. If you are like me, your life sometimes gets off track. I have made wrong decisions and terrible mistakes. Faithful friends do not abandon us. They help to restore the goodness and kindness they see in us. They do not tire of reminding us of humility, forgiveness and reconciliation. Faithful friends have the courage and honesty to tell us of our failures. They are lovingly frank when we are unfair, arrogant or full of pride.

Having a circle of faithful friends is a way to a deep and intimate encounter with the living Christ. When I became a religious missionary, I learned the meaning and essence of friendship more profoundly. It is the friendship in Jesus. In John 15:13-16, Jesus told his disciples, "No one has greater love than this, to lay down one's life for one's friends. You are my friends if you do what I command you. I no longer call you slaves, because a slave does not know what his master is doing. I have called you friends, because I have told you everything I have heard from my Father. It was not you who chose me, but I who chose you and appointed you to go and bear fruit that will remain, so that whatever you ask the Father in my name he may give you."

Friendship in Christ is eternal and filled with love. Jesus is the faithful friend who seeks and finds us untiringly, most especially in times of adversity, affliction and misfortune. Friendship in Christ is built on a strong foundation that protects and sustains us; it is the priceless treasure that no amount of anything else can balance; and it is a life-giving relationship that enables us to seek, find and share our friendships with others.

Jesus is the source and motivation for building a dynamic, healthy and lasting relationship with friends. Pope Francis reminds us that friendship is one of life's gifts and a grace from God.

While it is sad to geographically be away from my dearest friends due to my missionary life, I am grateful for the many new friendships with the people I have met in different countries with diverse cultures, beliefs, traditions and values. Through the various social network platforms, my faithful friends and I live out the promise that Jesus told his disciples, his friends, "I am with you always, to the very end of the age" (Matthew 28:20).

-------------------- 📖 --------------------

Words from Saint Arnold Janssen

"It costs us very much in our self-conquest to always be friendly towards others. These self-conquests are much more pleasing to the dear God than acts of exterior self-denial. These exterior acts have value only if they are done because of love."

For reflection
- What teachings of Christ do I keep and observe as foundations for my friendships with others?
- In what ways do I utilize social media in evangelization?
- How do I proclaim Christ's Good News in the "digital society"?

Generation Z and spiritual companions

What is All Saints' Day? How many Catholics remember that November 1 is a holy day of obligation? Young people who belong to Generation Z (those born after 1993) might not even know that there is a day to recognize and honor the lives and works of saints, both known and unknown.

Some people claim that saints are irrelevant in today's fast-paced, high-tech and secularized society. The influence of advertising has urged Generation Z to strive to follow their most-admired personalities on social media. They want to know all the nitty-gritty details about the personal lives of celebrities—the more personal the details, the better.

For Catholics of all generations, however, saints of yore and even contemporary saints can be admired personalities from whom we benefit by learning of their virtuous lives. Devotion to saints can grow from understanding the Apostles' Creed, a component of the Catholic Mass. Let us not simply say, "I believe in the communion of saints" without a deeper knowledge of its meaning.

The term "saints" encompasses the church's triumphant (all the souls in heaven), the church's suffering (the souls in purgatory), and the church's militant (those of us who are still on earth, aiming at sanctity). The unique and special communion depicts and upholds the sense of an all-embracing and belongingness in the community God.

We are all called to partake in the universal call for holiness, especially those who are here on earth. In a 2014 General Audience, Pope Francis said, "It is by living with love and offering Christian witness in our daily tasks that we are called to become saints.... Always and everywhere you can become a saint, that is, by being receptive to the grace that is working in us and leads us to holiness."

Studies about Generation Z indicate that they seek something that enables them to feel like they are making a difference in the world. Responding to the call of holiness is indeed a way to make a difference. Why not take the path of saints? Here are some ideas:

Let a saint be part of your life. Each life story of a saint gives us profound and inspiring thoughts on how to serve and follow God. There are many free apps, such as The Saint of the Day, that offer short and easy-to-read information about the life and work of a saint. Find out which aspects of the saint's life you could relate to such as the things you have in common or how the saint developed his/her relationship with God.

Be unique. Nowadays, being unique is trendy. How about making your prayer life unique? Saint Teresa of Avila offers writings on how to develop and grow in our prayer life. Saint Ignatius of Loyola teaches us the way of discernment. Embrace global diversity by following Saint Francis Xavier who shows us how to deal with challenges in foreign missions. Feel lost and don't know how to move forward from a dark past? Saint John of the Cross enlightens us on how to deal with dark and painful experiences. Saints are human beings, who like us, had joys, sorrows, weaknesses and problems during their times on earth. We can learn a lot from the saints.

Visit a parish. Most parishes have a patron saint whose feast day is celebrated annually. Celebrating the feast of the patron saint of a parish helps not only to strengthen the identity of the parish, but it gives parishioners knowledge about the life and works of the saint, which can help them grow in their own Christian faith. If there is an opportunity, visit the sacred and religious sites that are significant in the lives of the saints, such as their birthplaces, churches where they were baptized, schools where they studied, communities where they worked, shrines, tombs, and other sites consecrated for worship or ritual.

Go on a pilgrimage. These are also awe-inspiring places connected to saints where they were born, baptized, educated, worked or buried. Other sacred places mark where miracles or visions were reported. Seeing these places in person help us deepen our belief that a life in holiness is possible. One example is the Camino de Santiago, a pilgrimage to the Shrine of Saint James the Great in Galicia, Spain. In Portugal, you can visit the Sanctuary of Our Lady of Fatima, where Pope Francis recently canonized Jacinta and Francisco, two of the three children who witnessed the apparition of the Blessed Virgin Mary. In North America, you can visit Saint Anne de Beaupré Basilica in Quebec, the National Shrine of St. John Neumann in Philadelphia, the National Shrine of St. Frances Xavier Cabrini in Chicago or the National Shrine of Blessed Francis Xavier Seelos in New Orleans.

Pray through the intercession of saints. As the Catechism of the Catholic Church conveys, the saints in heaven are much closer to God than those of us still on earth. "The merciful love of God and his saints is always attentive to our prayers." (No. 962) Therefore, we ask our family and friends in heaven to pray for us, to hand deliver our prayers to God.

Borrow from the saints. Sometimes, we are overwhelmed by the trials we face in life. We seek words to articulate our thoughts and express our feelings. During those times, we can express our petition to God through the prayers of saints, such as "make me an instrument of your peace," a prayer attributed to St. Francis of Assisi. When we are frightened and terrified by darkness in our society, let us pray with St. Arnold Janssen, the founder of the Society of the Divine Word and two communities of religious women: "May the darkness of sin and night of unbelief vanish before the light of the Word and the spirit of grace, and may the heart of Jesus live in the hearts of all. Amen."

Sainthood comes to those who selflessly offered their lives to God. Members of Generation Z are characterized as self-starters and more accepting of others. To them, I say, why not include a saint in your life? Accept what a saint can offer you and be transformed. Regardless of generation, with the grace of God, let us all strive to live out our call to be saints here on earth.

--------------------- 📖 ---------------------
Words from Saint Arnold Janssen
"The saints knew how to live their faith: they recognized in it nothing that was simply an exterior act, but [they saw] the holy will of God. God the Lord gladly sees this when we decisively fulfill his holy will in our lives."

For reflection
- Do I pray to God through the intercession of the saints?
- Do I use devotional prayers in order to make my encounter with God more reverent and intimate?
- Given a chance, where would I go for a pilgrimage?

Presence in sacred waiting

When I was six, I had an unforgettable experience that left an imprint on me. Due to miscommunication, my parents failed to pick me up after school.

I would have risked going home by myself, but it was already dark and I did not know the way. I was terribly scared. This event happened in the days before cellphones. The school office was closed. I had no choice other than to wait.

I did not cry. However, I felt helpless and alone. That childhood experience impacted my attitude growing up. My trust became fragile. Consequently, I developed the "I'm in charge" and let me handle it" attitude. I became independent to a fault. I took control and manipulated situations to avoid anxiety in waiting.

There are moments throughout our lives when we find ourselves waiting in frustration. Despite our efforts for better outcomes, we feel stuck in situations that nobody wants. Inasmuch as we want to quickly ease the pain we face, we find ourselves lost, not knowing how to manage ourselves.

People who recently have relationship breakups struggle; they sometimes need time to help them regain their self-worth. Individuals recovering from addiction tussle to keep themselves sober. Families with a seriously ill member sometimes fight with one another due to financial burdens, care-giving concerns and emotional distress. With a desire to give their children a better life, many single parents are exhausted, having two jobs to make ends meet.

Often, it's impossible to fix our life problems in a short time span. We sometimes have to struggle under agonizing circumstances for quite a while. The perplexity of everyday life might make us doubt the presence of God. We might live as if there is no God.

The season of Advent is a sacred waiting period. When observed, the season makes us aware of our ongoing journey into a deeper reality. We can learn how to travel the journey with the examples of our faith models in the Advent narratives, people who prayerfully experienced sacred waiting.

In the Gospel of Luke, the old Zechariah and Elizabeth felt hopelessness while waiting to have a child. Yet, they remained righteous in the sight of God, observing all the Lord's commands and decrees. After waiting for a long time, an angel sent by God said: *"Do not be afraid, Zechariah, because your prayer has been heard. Your wife Elizabeth will bear you a son, and you shall name him John"* (Luke 1:13). Zechariah, Elizabeth and John show us the divine work of God in a family who stays together in sacred waiting.

Joseph may have been disillusioned, resentful and afraid when he learned of Mary's pregnancy. He could have followed his immediate plan of quietly sending her away. Instead, he took time to discern. In a dream, an angel of God told him, *"Joseph, son of David, do not be afraid to take Mary your wife into your home. For it is through the Holy Spirit that this child has been conceived in her. She will bear a son and you are to name him Jesus, because he will save his people from their sins"* (Matthew 1:20-21). He gained courage to follow God's salvation plan.

Mary opened herself to God's will by accepting the Archangel Gabriel's words, *"Do not be afraid, Mary, for you have found favor with God. Behold, you will conceive in your womb and bear a son, and you shall name him Jesus"* (Luke 1:30-31). Selflessly, Mary said yes to God's call. Her acceptance of God's will encourages us to wait in confident assurance. Regardless of the difficulties that lie ahead, God will never abandon us.

We might be afraid of the uncertainty. Advent reminds us not to be afraid to bring ourselves before God. We are invited to recognize again God's existence.

We are summoned to reflect and be present in sacred waiting. As we journey through the Advent season, let us bring our minds, hearts and spirits into contemplative awareness before God. When we bring our worries and burdens to God, time is nothing.

Theologian Ronald Rolheiser wrote, "To give birth to what's divine requires the slow patience of gestation." Advent has come. Spend time to reflect on your meaningful experiences of waiting. Pray to God for help in recognizing his divine presence in your sacred waiting.

Words from Saint Arnold Janssen

"Patience and trust in the Lord guard us from anxiety and over-eagerness to take on tasks before the right hour has come."

For reflection
- What are the areas of my life where I need to grow in patience?
- How attentive am I to God in my prayers?

Art of waiting for busy people

Advent, the period when Catholics prepare for the birth of our Lord and reflect on the Second Coming of Christ, is a time of great anticipatory joy. However, it also can be a challenge for those of us who aren't practiced in the art of waiting.

Most people don't want to be on a waiting list. We have developed a rush-hour mentality—expecting swift messaging, express shipping, instant cooking recipes, high-speed Internet connections and quick passes to avoid long lines in amusement parks. Many of us have short attention spans.

Due to our preoccupation, we don't always notice how our fast-paced, high-tech world has conditioned our minds to accomplish tasks as quickly as possible. This season, let us purposefully slow down and reflect.

Let the Good News lead to a healthier lifestyle. Allow me to share some of the practices that I hope will help make your Advent journey a blessed one.

Visit someone who longs for your presence and needs your service. After receiving the good news from the Archangel Gabriel, our Blessed Mother Mary went to her cousin Elizabeth to share the joy of being chosen to bear the Son of God. Mary stayed with Elizabeth, who also was pregnant. She went not only because she longed to see her cousin but also to provide assistance to her. Presence with service is one of the best gifts we can offer to others. You can bestow the gift of presence upon a family member, friend or colleague. Or you can go to a prison, hospital, senior home, orphanage or homeless center.

Keep a daily Advent journal. In the Bible, prior to the Annunciation, prophets foretold the birth of Jesus, the Messiah. Jeremiah prophesied of the Messiah. Isaiah spoke about the ruler. Micah said that the Messiah would be born in Bethlehem. They are three among other prophets who foretold the birth of Jesus. In their writings, they described their deepest desires, longings and hopes for the coming of Jesus. We can do the same. We can crystalize our thoughts and feelings about our waiting and preparation for the coming of Jesus by journaling. Your journal entries can be as simple as a word, phrase or sentence. You may want to use a daily devotional book for Advent to guide you. Committing your excitement, frustrations, achievements and struggles to paper can deepen the experience of Advent.

Be imaginative and create your own Advent masterpiece. Joseph and Mary traveled to Bethlehem and looked for a place to stay. Other than that, we don't know much about their journey, their period of waiting and preparation for the birth of Jesus. However, Advent is full of signs and symbols with profound meanings: candles, wreaths, trees, stars. These symbols serve as windows to God. They give us a glimpse into the mystery of the Divine. Creating art can help you fill in the blanks. You can draw, paint, sculpt or crochet. During the process, reflect upon ways that you can welcome Jesus into your heart. Producing artwork can help you direct your mind and heart in the spirit of the season. God can transform these ordinary objects into gifts of grace. We, too, are transformed in making art. Try it! You may be surprised by what you can imagine.

Participate in an Advent retreat or reconciliation service. When Zechariah, Joseph and Mary encountered God's angels, each one responded with humility and acknowledged their unworthiness. Advent is time for us to reflect on renewing our relationship with God. It is an opportunity to look back and reflect on all the things that have happened throughout the year. Surely, there are many things that we did of which we are proud. There were also times when we stumbled in our lives, times that made us feel broken and unworthy. Local parishes often organize Advent retreats and common reconciliation services to help the faithful to prepare spiritually. Our participation is a great gift to Jesus.

Attend the Eucharist daily during Advent. The Scripture readings during Advent offer wisdom and understanding of our Christian faith life. We go to Mass not for pep talks and entertainment but for real-life transformation. We go to Mass not to feel good but to be blessed by God's goodness. Our presence in the Holy Eucharist is a sacred moment during which we experience inner connection between expectation and the fulfillment of our waiting. In the Eucharist, we see and feel Jesus' presence. It nurtures our longing and strengthens our hope. If we allow ourselves to remain still in the Eucharist, we realize that we are not waiting for Jesus' coming. Rather, Jesus is waiting for our response to His Divine love.

No matter how fast-paced and hectic our daily schedule, we should find time and seek occasions in which we can pause, breathe, wait and be blessed by God's grace. The Advent season offers time to slow down and the opportunity to experience waiting—preparing ourselves for Jesus in a profound and spiritual manner. May the grace of Advent be with us all!

-------------------- 📖 --------------------
Words from Saint Arnold Janssen
"Genuine meditative prayer is actually the offering and gift of ourselves to God in recognition of his greatness and our lowliness."

For reflection
- Have I developed a discipline in my prayer life?
- Do I seek guidance or accompaniment on my faith journey from a spiritual director, counselor, or mentor?
- What are the gifts that I receive through genuine meditative prayer?

Hearing Christ's coming through our beating hearts

Not too long ago, we began the Advent season. Now it's almost Christmas! The celebration of the birth of Christ Jesus. With our hearts, minds and spirits, we prepared ourselves for Christ so that we may be able to welcome him with joy.

Christ is our hope at this moment when we are bombarded with social conflicts, injustices and violence. That gift especially struck me during Advent Sunday Masses at the Special Religious Education Development (SPRED) center, a community of people with developmental disabilities.

I found myself deeply moved by the participation of my friends from SPRED in the offertory and preparation of the gifts at Mass. Despite their limitations, my friends participated and engaged in the Eucharistic celebration.

A father and son walked together to the sanctuary. They slowly and patiently placed a purple linen on the altar table. *A prayer pleading to Christ to cover our broken world with his mercy and love.*

A mother and son went to the altar, carrying a lit candle. *The divine light that we need to dispel the darkness in our society.*

A mother and daughter brought a vase of beautiful flowers to the altar. *A prayer to restore the beauty of creation so that we all may enjoy the nature that God has given us.*

A family of four offered the bread to the table. *An act that reminds all that the family that prays—asking God for their daily bread amid hunger, poverty and daily struggle—stays together.*

Then, another family walked to the altar, carrying the wine to be blessed and shared. *A symbolic prayer of a family who sought Jesus to quench their thirst for loving protection against pain, depression and spiritual crisis.*

The way each person performed his or her task in the liturgy was touching. My friends didn't let their intellectual and physical limitations hinder their participation in the celebration. They fulfilled their assigned roles with dedication and reverence.

People in the pews stayed still in awe. Each of us allowed ourselves to be immersed in silence. Our silence became our encounter with the sacred presence of Christ among us.

Sacred silence filled the assembly and radiated like the light of Christ. A sacred silence that gives joy and hope.
God became human on a silent night so that we could hear and feel his coming. his birth was not announced with loud sounds but rather through the beating of our hearts. God sent his son in the middle of darkness because Christ dispels darkness and illuminates our lives with his unconditional love.

The mystery of God becoming human is the source of grace that leads us to humility and trust. We must admit that we cannot make our world a better place by our own efforts.
We can only see God because God wills it. God wants to make our hearts anew by filling them with gratitude and hope. We need Christ's presence in our hearts. I noticed that my friends' relationships with Christ empower them and give them profound joy despite their disabilities.

Like my friends, we need a deeper, stronger and closer relationship with Christ. Christmas is our opportunity to renew our relationship with Christ. It is a grace-filled season that invites us to restore our way of life according to Christ's love.

It is a time to silence our hearts from the noise of our secular world. It is the season that urges us to listen to Christ and respond to his invitation to rest in our hearts.

We can only attain the lasting joy that Christmas gives us if we proclaim and live out the teachings of Christ in our daily lives. Let us share in Christ's birth by living in his light. Let us accept our brokenness, incompleteness and wounds.

Let us be like the shepherds who glorify and praise God for all the things they heard and saw at Jesus' birth. His coming to be with us is the Good News! Let us share the love of Christ this Christmas!

---------------------- 📖 ----------------------

Words from Saint Arnold Janssen

"How much fullness in spiritual and bodily blessings has the Christ Child brought here on earth. Let us be grateful to him. Let us make others aware of the blessings he desires to share with us."

For reflection

- In what ways do I recognize and uphold the human dignity and rights of people with disabilities in the church, workplace and public areas?
- What lessons do people with disabilities teach me about myself and about God?

How liturgy and worship fostered my religious missionary vocation

Nearly 20 years into the new millennium, society sometimes asks how modern young people choose the religious life. A summer school course at Catholic Theological Union gave me cause to reflect and recall my own liturgical formation–learning the holy work of God–from the age of four and how it shaped the foundation of my vocation.

My parents seized the opportunity to foster my gift of faith. I was baptized at Saint Rafael Parish in Pasay City, Philippines. They sent me to the parish's preschool where I had my first religious education. I believe that my baptism and early education sowed the seeds of my religious vocation.

I remember three significant experiences in that parish: the pouring of holy water on my head during baptism; Easter Sunday celebration where an image of Judas Iscariot was burned in effigy; and the moment when I realized I wanted to be like the altar servers and wear the vestments of the priest.

When I moved to elementary school, I was fortunate to receive religious education in a non-Catholic private school where I first experienced the Sacrament of Reconciliation and received my First Communion. During high school, I joined and became a leader of a Catholic youth ministry.

Salesian brothers and priests lived in our community. They did youth ministry in our small urban settlement. Every weekend, the seminarians visited our place for catechism class. They helped us establish our chapel and develop our community parish activities.

I became one of the youths who made parish activities a recreational part of our community. We were involved as parish ministers, such as choir member, altar server, commentator and lector.

I read the Bible and adopted religious practices like novenas and devotion to the Blessed Mother and Santo Niño (Child Jesus). As children, we raised awareness and promoted the Catholic faith by organizing social outreach projects. For the feast of our patron saint, we organized activities, such as a procession, sports festival and a Bible quiz bee. After earning a bachelor's degree in religious education from a Catholic university, I became a religion teacher.

I am thankful for the rich experience of parish involvement at a very young age. I owe it to my family, the parish community and the people I met in school. The music, gestures, Scriptures, prayers of the faithful and Eucharistic prayers became an integral part of my growth as a baptized child who was exploring the mystery of sacred experience. It taught me a sense of community, belonging, diversity, inclusion, reconciliation, peace, justice and charity.

My presence in the liturgy was not as a watcher but as a participant who was being transformed by the living God. As stated in the Congregation for Divine Worship's *Directory for Masses with Children*, worship teaches human values through "the community activity, exchange of greetings, capacity to listen and to seek and grant pardon, expression of gratitude, experience of symbolic actions, a meal of friendship, and festive celebration."

Through Mass, I learned active, conscious and authentic participation in the Eucharistic celebration. Furthermore, I witnessed the dynamic life of the Gospels, the Word of God. Over the years, as I grow in age and wisdom, my ears have been trained to the sounds of the words in Scripture verses.

When I listen to a lector, I understand that it is not a mere reading of Scripture. It is the proclamation of the Divine Word. It became the lamp unto my feet and a light unto my path (Psalm 119:105).

From my first encounter with the living God in worship to where I am at right now, the liturgy has formed my baptismal identity as a child of God. The proclaimed Word that I heard during the liturgy grew within me. It is constantly calling forth an ever deeper spiritual response. It leads me to unlimited possibilities for an encounter with God through worship and the liturgy.

Words from Saint Arnold Janssen

"Your heart should be like an altar on which the sacrifice of thankfulness may always rise up to God."

For reflection
- What were my childhood experiences that brought me closer to God?
- In what ways do I show that I have an active, full and conscious participation in the liturgy?
- How do I nurture my vocation through the liturgy?

Let our children come to us

While preparing for my class on worship with children, I read an article about Pope Francis in which he said that children's tears are the "best sermon." He explained that "children cry, they are noisy, they don't stop moving. But it really irritates me when I see a child crying in church and someone says they must go out. God's voice is in a child's tears: they must never be kicked out of church."

Jesus said, "Let the children come to me, and do not prevent them; for the kingdom of heaven belongs to such as these" (Matthew 19:14).

This passage always comes to mind when I see parents struggling to calm a child during Mass. I admit that I am one of those worshipers who labors to keep my composure and focus on the celebration when there is a crying or playing child at the liturgy.

A child's awe and wonder, a gift of the Holy Spirit, is a divine source of their desire to be in relationship with our God.

There were instances when the presence of a disruptive child became a cause of division within the worshiping community. Parents are in a dilemma whether to bring their child with them to fulfill their Sunday obligation or to let them participate in the Mass only when they learn to behave themselves. Perhaps, we should ask ourselves: Which option is better? A church full of crying children or a quiet and empty church?

As baptized Christians, we have a shared responsibility in molding children's engagement in the liturgy. We have to accompany and guide them on their paths as they discover the beauty and gifts of the liturgy.

Children's participation should not be something taken as added attendance in the assembly or to merely make the celebration more festive. Everyone must realize that the presence of a child in the liturgy is an essential gift to the whole community.

It gives life to the community. A child cannot and should not be excluded from worship. It reminds us of our interdependence with one another.

In the liturgy, children need us, and we need them. Joan Patano Vos writes, "the role of adults in the church is not to 'put' God into children. Rather, we help to shape an environment where they feel at home and in and with the divine presence. And then we need to pray with them."

Children remind us of the sacredness of our humanity. A child's knowledge of liturgy does not come from a database. As children grow up and become members of the worshiping community, we need to help them realize their God-given gifts. We should encourage them to use those gifts to the fullest.

We need to guide them in sharing their gifts with the whole community. Parents who let their children be present and participate in the Mass affirm those gifts.

As Diane Apostolos-Cappadona writes, "the child learns to worship through experience from the very first moments in the church. The child's first 'understandings' come through the senses: one sees the flickering candles, the smoke of incense, and the colorful movement of celebrants in procession; one hears the music of the choir and the chanting priests and readers; one kisses icons, the cross, the gospel book...one feels one's head anointed with oil or splashed with water; and one tastes the wine and bread of holy communion. By age two, children will be imitating many of the things seen and heard."

We have to be patient, kind, understanding and loving with our children as they take time to grasp and express faith in worship the way we hope they will. A child's awe and wonder, a gift of the Holy Spirit, is a divine source of their desire to be in relationship with our God.

-------------------- 📖 --------------------

Words from Saint Arnold Janssen

"We are really children of God. As parents let their children take part in their heritage, so God also does this with us. In Holy Baptism the heavenly Father has taken us up as his children since we are to take part in the heritage of heaven."

For reflection

- In what ways do I welcome children in the church, promote their welfare, and keep them safe and free to worship according to their capacity?
- How do I participate in the efforts of our parish community in creating an environment that will provide opportunities for children to develop their faith in God?

The excellence of love

A week before the profession of perpetual vows—the ceremony in which my confreres and I pledge to live in poverty, obedience and chastity for the rest of our lives—I had an opportunity to reflect upon 1 Corinthians 13. I asked myself two questions: When did I learn about the religious vows? How did I first learn the ways of living out the vows? These two questions led me to recall three regular occasions when I was a child.

Poverty

My family lived in relative poverty in Manila. During family mealtime, my mom taught my brothers and me to put only a small serving of food on our plates. We learned that the food must be shared. After everyone received a portion, then and only then could we take another serving. My brothers and I shared not only food but also clothes, school supplies and shoes. Through this family condition, I learned about poverty.

Obedience

The second occasion was doing household chores. My mom was dependent upon me to maintain orderliness and keep the house clean. I cooked, prepared our table for meals, swept and scrubbed the floor and did laundry. When my mom went to work, she told me what needed to be done. I paid attention. I even wrote her instructions on a sheet of paper so I wouldn't forget anything. I learned obedience.

Chastity

The third occasion was taking care of my younger brothers. My mom taught me to love my younger brothers by taking care of them. When they were little children, I changed diapers, bathed, fed and played with them. I brought them to and from school and helped them with their homework. I spent most of my childhood taking care of my brothers. We developed a brotherly relationship. I learned about love.

False promises

Life changed when I became a young adult. I sought independence. I demanded freedom. After high school graduation at age 17, I walked away from my family.

After finishing university studies, I earned a good salary as a teacher. I could buy almost anything I wanted. I became self-serving with no need to worry about sharing. I had my own place. I managed it according to my own way.

I met many people in the teaching field. Some of the people whom I thought of as friends had questionable values. I ignored my inner voice that warned me because I longed for acceptance and a sense of belonging. I found myself trapped in unhealthy relationships. I cultivated shallow connections.

An authentic life

Fortunately, my life changed again at age 30. I entered the Society of the Divine Word with a strong desire to leave my old life behind. Formation has led me to a deeper understanding of the religious vows and to a stronger conviction to live out my life according to God's holy will.

I have learned a meaningful life in the state of consecrated celibacy through personal friendship with Christ, living faith, fraternal sharing in community and selfless dedication to be committed to our vocation. In our community, we strive to form a true brotherhood, where every confrere can feel at home, form deep friendships and find fulfillment in his work and development of his talents.

Our shared mission calls us generously to place time, talents, work, and community goods at the service of our missionary task. By virtue of the vow of poverty, we strive to bind ourselves to a simple lifestyle. It enables us to accept our dependence on God and become inwardly free and detached from all earthly goods and honors. We become available and open to God and others.

In a world where so many seek to impose their will upon others, we seek to learn our vow of obedience in order to uphold unity in community. Our obedience unites us, helping us to focus on our society's missionary goals.

Through Christ's love

As I look back and reflect on my past, I am able to heartily echo the words of St. Paul to the Corinthians, "When I was a child, I used to speak like a child, think like a child, reason like a child; when I became a man, I did away with childish things (1 Cor 13:11)."

With joy and gratitude during the perpetual vows ceremony, I uttered those words: "I solemnly promise you—Father, Son and Holy Spirit—to live for life chastity, poverty, and obedience, according to the Constitutions of the Society of the Divine Word."

The love of Christ urges me to be prudent, worthy and responsible in carrying out missionary service with joy and gratitude. Through Christ's love, each of us is able to bear all things, believe all things, hope all things and endure all things.

---------------------- 📖 ----------------------

Words from Saint Arnold Janssen

"With humility we want to live up to the commitment we have made in our profession. We honor our profession by being one in heart and mind with our confreres."

For reflection

- What can I do today to love others more fully just as Jesus wants me to?

A marathon, a faith journey and the abounding grace of God

It's the beginning of a new decade. I like to spend time looking back and reflecting on the many things that transpired. One such event was my first marathon. During the race, the energy of the crowd was contagious. It motivated runners like me to persevere and reach the finish line.

A marathon is much like a faith journey. Both can make us question if we can finish the race. Both can fulfill a heart's desire. Both are pursued from an inner call and can compel us to leave a beloved homeland (or a beloved couch).

When I decided to enter the Society of the Divine Word, I sought something greater than myself, something that at the time was unclear to me. I was sad to leave family and friends, yet the prospects also filled me with excitement.

Running a marathon is like the race of faith. Faith in Christ gives us the courage to go to unknown places and to be with strangers. On the marathon route, you also find yourself among strangers.

Following a friend's suggestion, I wore a shirt with my name on it. I was surprised and elated by people who cheered me on, calling my name at the top of their lungs. I heard my name loud and clear. The name on my chest made the people notice me, an average runner, small in stature, among roughly 45,000 runners. The loud cheer was like an energy drink that helped me finish the race.

Reaching the finish line was exhilarating, much like the way I imagine Zacchaeus felt when Jesus called him by name (Luke 19:1-10). Zacchaeus' small stature did not hinder him from seeing and meeting Jesus. As the chief publican, or tax collector, Zacchaeus was a wealthy collaborator of the hated Roman occupiers. He exploited his own people. Because of his ill repute, he hesitated to approach the Master. His effort to see Jesus clearly led him to change his heart and his life.

In one of Pope Francis's homilies, the pontiff said, "even today we can risk not getting close to Jesus because we don't feel big enough, because we don't think ourselves worthy. This is a great temptation; it has to do not only with self-esteem but with faith itself. For faith tells us that we are children of God…that is what we are."

I can relate to Zacchaeus. With a contemplative mind, I followed a path guided by Scriptures in a way that has been spiritually meaningful. During my silent prayer, I heard God cheering me on. God awakened my spirit and lifted me up from brooding caused by past injuries. God's loving presence opened my heart and motivated me to start over.

Christ continues to invite us on the faith journey. Like a marathon, it will not be easy. There will be doubts and confusion, discouragement and disappointments, frustrations and limitations, yet Jesus' encounter with Zacchaeus offers us three ways to run the race called the Christian life.

First, when Jesus came to Jericho, passing through the town, Zacchaeus, due to his physical limitation, climbed a sycamore tree in order to see Jesus. **Let us persist, strive and persevere to seek and find Jesus especially when he is passing through our daily lives.** Jesus comes through people and event around us. A listening heart is a key to noticing Jesus.

Second, Jesus looked up the sycamore tree and said, "Zacchaeus, come down quickly, for today I must stay at your house" (Luke 19:5-6). Zacchaeus came down and received him with joy. **Let us deepen our encounters with Jesus by receiving and loving him with joy.** The way to receive Jesus and express our love for him is by contemplating the Good News proclaimed to us, especially in the sacraments, such as in the Eucharist and reconciliation. We can only deepen our encounter with Jesus by making a dwelling place in our hearts. Let the Divine Word remain in our hearts.

Third, Zacchaeus said to the Lord, "Behold, half of my possessions, Lord, I shall give to the poor, and if I have extorted anything from anyone I shall repay it four times over" (Luke 19:8). **Let us concretize the love we have in our relationship with Jesus through acts of charity.** Our relationship with Jesus will only be possible through interconnectedness and interdependence with others through acts of service.

The three responses of Zacchaeus to Jesus are examples for us to imitate. We do not know how the upcoming years will unfold. Let us prepare ourselves to face many questions, doubts and difficulties in our Christian faith lives. Let our hearts remain attentive to the call of Jesus. In other words, to run alone is a race, but to run with God is grace.

Words from Saint Arnold Janssen

"Go forward with full trust in God and resolve again to build up your life in holy humility, and thus God the Lord will be with you."

For reflection

- How do I use my God-given gift to know and follow Christ?
- What are the challenges that I would like to bring to Christ for guidance and wisdom?

Emotional memory of God

Every year, members of the Divine Word Techny community, the Theologate community, novices and friends gather to celebrate St. John's Night. It's an annual tradition in honor of the Divine Word as depicted by Saint John the Evangelist.

In the previous year, we had a wonderful time singing Christmas carols as part of the entertainment. This year, we also played three simple games. The first game was called "Name that Christmas Carol."

It's a game that involved their sense of memory. As the emcee, I gave them a set of words in random order that corresponded to the title of a given Christmas song. They had to tell the correct and complete song title.

The second game involved their sense of hearing. It's called "That Noise Sounds Familiar." They had to listen attentively in order to recognize and tell the various sounds they frequently heard in their surroundings, such as the flushing of a toilet bowl, a vacuum cleaner, someone snoring or someone drinking water.

For the last game, called "Mystery Box," they use the sense of touch to guess several items—a table napkin, a packet of ketchup, and salt and pepper shakers—hidden inside a box. The elders especially enjoyed playing the games.

The activities exceeded my expectations. I was worried when I was preparing the games because I was concerned whether they would be able to participate and enjoy the games. I thought that some of them might not know the song title because of their difficulty remembering. Others have trouble hearing, and some are dealing with involuntary movements and mobility.

What I witnessed during our Saint John's Night celebration is the embodiment of the Scriptures in 1 John 4:12-13 that reads, "No one has seen God at any time; if we love one another, God abides in us, and His love is perfected in us. By this we know that we abide in Him and He in us, because He has given us of His Spirit."

The quality of life of our retired confreres, with their daily concerns and struggles, led me to a different perspective of mission. The idea that they are not doing any full-time ministry or active missionary work in a parish or in another country could be taken by others as having a lifestyle of ease and leisure.

I agree with author Peter Van Breeman when he wrote "all who genuinely live their mission experience an inner freedom." In his book *The God Who Won't Let Go,* he points out three crucial ways for deepening the mission. It clearly describes how our retired confreres carry out their mission.

First, they allot quality time for prayer. Second, they pay attention to their ongoing human development that lead them to learning about themselves. Third, they grow in a discipline that leads them more and more toward basic integrity.

The smiles on their faces and the laughter that filled our dining hall during the celebration made me realize one more admirable trait of my elderly confreres: their spirit of childlike piety.

Even though many older Divine Word confreres acknowledge their limitation of memory and physical abilities, their emotional memory of God still gives them great joy. They find that their daily prayers and liturgy in the community continuously awaken their memory of God.

While they struggle with a loss of hearing that forces them to depend on hearing-aid devices, they are attentively listening to God whom they believe is communicating with them through their daily lives. Their unwavering trust in God is manifested in their ability to listen and follow God's will even in the midst of daily struggles.

While their physical immobility seriously limits their capacity to move independently, it is fascinating how their ability to connect with others—through personal and intimate daily encounters with the people around them—becomes their gift to the community. Their physical limitations don't lessen their sense of sincere gratitude when they shake hands or embrace others to show their appreciation and care.

In order to love our neighbors with a perfect heart, we have to let our memory of God's unconditional love awaken in us! To see God's presence in our maddening society, loud and noisy, we are called to pay attention with a listening heart. To keep God remaining in us, we have to embody the spirit of surrendering to God's divine will.

--------------------- 📖 --------------------

Words from Saint Arnold Janssen

"How much fullness in spiritual and bodily blessings has the Christ Child brought here to earth. Let us be grateful to Him. Let us make others aware of the blessings He desires to share with us."

For reflection
- What in my life awakens my memory of God?
- In what ways do I surrender myself to God's divine will?

Sharing sacred space with the marginalized

"Ministry is, first of all, receiving God's blessing from those to whom we minister. What is this blessing? It is a glimpse of the face of God." These words of Henri Nouwen resonate with my experience in the Special Religious Development (SPRED) ministry of the Archdiocese of Chicago. SPRED is a program of faith formation designed to meet the spiritual needs of people with intellectual, developmental and learning disabilities.

On a Tuesday afternoon, a few hours before our first SPRED session of the year, I received a phone call from our lead catechist. She informed me about a new friend who would be coming and asked if I would accompany her in our group. I was asked to take the role of a helper catechist, unlike in the past when I simply observed the whole group during a session.

I felt excited and nervous at the same time. This would be my first time in the role of a helper catechist in our SPRED group. When I arrived at the SPRED center that evening, I felt apprehensive. My heart was beating fast as I entered our preparation room. Our activity catechist welcomed me and introduced me to Marie, the friend whom I was to accompany.

As we approached, Marie was playing with sand in the corner of our preparation room. She looked at me for a second and then offered her right hand to shake my hand. I told her my name and smiled as we shook hands. She does not communicate verbally. She is on the autism spectrum. I was not quite sure how I was going to build a relationship with a person who was nonverbal.

After shaking hands with Marie, I pulled up a chair and sat across from her at the table. I sat with her as she quietly worked with sand and seashells in a large container. She scooped the sand with a small shell and poured it like a flowing waterfall. While she held the shell in her left hand to scoop and pour the sand, she was catching and pouring sand with her right hand. She was attentively focused on the sand as she worked.

My anxiousness started to gradually subside. I believe her calming presence helped me get over my anxiety. She was at ease and did not disrupt any of the others during the whole session. She did not walk away from me, and I observed from her behavior that she wanted to spend time with me. I believe we were both comfortable with one another. I was grateful and joyful that we were able to bond at our first meeting. It gave me hope that her presence and involvement in our first session would be beneficial for her whole faith formation.

In our SPRED community, many parents have shared stories about their sad and painful experiences of rejection and isolation because of their child's condition. These stories convey a social reality—that disabilities can lead to being isolated and marginalized. Through no fault of their own or their families, our friends sometimes are marginalized in parish settings despite church documents that uphold their belonging to the family of God.

Many families were discouraged from attending the Sunday liturgy with their family member with disabilities because of the ways they have been treated by others in the assembly. There have been occasions when people with disabilities and their families were reprimanded and asked to leave the church because others could not cope with some of the difficulties the person with disabilities was having.

These are pressing issues that we attempt to address throughout our catechist formation in SPRED. As catechists, we advocate for the rights of people with disabilities to share the liturgy with all believers. The faith formation empowers them to truly belong in our liturgical communities. Through our SPRED community of faith, our friends become more comfortable entering into the worship experience of the whole church.

Parish leaders need to be sensitive and listen attentively. Patience, respect and collaboration are necessary both on the part of the family requesting support and on the part of the parish trying to be supportive.

Some people ask: Are they capable of having faith? Can they acquire faith and explain it? Are they capable of knowing their religion? Do they understand the meaning of prayers, hymns, gestures and sacraments? Can they really participate in liturgy?

Our friends with disabilities may not have the same cognitive capacity as we have to understand prayers, hymns, gestures and sacraments, but we have to understand that faith is neither fundamentally abstract nor purely conceptual. It is about relationships. For that reason, persons with intellectual and developmental disabilities can be educated in faith by providing them the opportunity to experience our faith.

Each person is a human being. Each person has his or her own way of relating to others. Abstract or conceptual knowing may be limited, but there are other ways of knowing, such as symbolic or intuitive knowing and response. Our friends have a strong affective capacity to make others feel valued. Let the relationship they share with us, the friendship, our experience together in SPRED become the vehicle for their physical, psychological and spiritual growth.

At a Mass in Rome, Pope Francis told those in the audience that when St. Pius X ruled in 1910 that children as young as seven years old could receive Communion, similar objections were raised. "But that child won't understand," the critics complained. But St. Pius went ahead, knowing: "Each one of us has a different way of understanding things. One understands one way and another in a different manner, but we can all know God."

One of our fellow catechists shared this reflection: "SPRED means creating bonds of new friendships, a beautiful sense of community, learning to see Christ in everyday situations, knowing that I need a Shepherd; not being afraid to grow, to love, to forgive; seeing my friend with disabilities for the first time lean forward with her hands outstretched to hear what Jesus wants to say to her today."

Every Sunday I see Marie with her mom, dad and grandmother at our liturgy at the SPRED center. I admire them for their love and dedication as they accompany her on her faith journey. I also am inspired by Marie who does not merely attend the liturgy but also participates according to her own capacity. When I see her, I remember how she leads me during our SPRED sessions with her reflective presence, her deep awareness and loving attentiveness to others.

Words of Saint Arnold Janssen

"Since the dear God has poured out the fullness of his love over us, God also wants us to be friendly and loving towards each other. 'A new commandment I give you, that you love one another' (John 13:34)."

For reflection
- What is the role of faith in my relationship with others?
- How do I promote disability awareness and acceptance in my community?

The joy, beauty and goodness of Christ's peace

A few weeks before we recommenced with our SPRED session, our SPRED catechists' team received the news that our leader catechist couldn't continue her role anymore. We believe that she really wanted to remain in her role in our group. However, she needed to take a break in order to be with her family, especially with her mom who was sick.

Our whole team decided that I would take the role of leader catechist. I had mixed emotions on the evening of our session. I was excited and nervous. Also, I was a little bit worried because part of taking the role of leader catechist is that I would no longer be a helper catechist to Marie. I had the pleasure and privilege of accompanying her as helper catechist for a year and half in our group. A new helper catechist joined our group to take over this role as a new helper catechist for Marie. We were very delighted and thankful that our new catechist would become part of our friendship, especially with Marie. However, we anticipated that it would take time for Marie and her new helper catechist to get to know each other. Marie would again undergo again transition and adjustment.

We, the catechists, prepared ourselves for the return of our friends. All our friends have many gifts that we are discovering continuously. We knew that there were many things that transpired with them during the two months' break.

As a leader catechist, I stayed next to the entrance and welcomed our friends. Andrea is a tenderhearted girl who is friendly and sweet. Andrew is an observant, straightforward boy. Daniel, who is constantly enthusiastic, is animated and loving. Leah, a quiet girl with a calming presence, has a contagious smile. Fred is a gentleman, polite and intelligent. Mary is a goodhearted girl whose gentleness and genuineness draws us closer to her. They are ages 11 to 16. They are on different levels in terms of their developmental and intellectual growth.

Our activity catechist prepared the activity room and filled it with sensorial materials, such as paints, puzzles, sandboxes, musical instruments and coloring books. They helped our friends get in touch with their senses. As the youth entered the room, they approach each other one by one. We shook hands and gave warm welcomes. The catechists try to make all of them feel safe and loved.

On one occasion, I gazed at them from my seat while they were doing their chosen activities in silence. I was drawn to their calming presence. The love and peace of our Lord Jesus Christ was with us.

The sense of peace became deeper and stronger when we went to our sacred space, a room where we gather around the Holy Bible that is placed on a small table at the center. Next to it was a vase of fresh flowers and a lighted candle. Together with those objects before our eyes, the dim lighting made us feel the sacredness of our gathering.

Our goal that evening was to ponder our experience of peace. I showed two different images of snow-covered countryside. One was a painting, and the other was a photograph. We shared our personal experiences of how the snow during winter made us feel peace.

As I was showing the painting and photograph to each of our friends, I was surprised that a few of them touched the images. Perhaps their sense of touch was evoked in them by the images. As some of them touched the images, they thought they would feel the cold snow. In our sharing, we related our experience of peace with the sense of peace in our liturgy, when we go to church.

Our celebration in the sacred room gave us a deep joy, especially when we shared our thoughts and feelings. I stood and proclaimed the Scriptures from Philippians 4:4-7, "Rejoice in the Lord always. I shall say it again: rejoice! Your kindness should be known to all. The Lord is near. Have no anxiety at all, but in everything, by prayer and petition, with thanksgiving, make your requests known to God. Then the peace of God that surpasses all understanding will guard your hearts and minds in Christ Jesus."

We felt Christ's presence in our midst when the Scripture passage was proclaimed to us. We opened ourselves to Christ speaking to us, because Christ Himself is with us.

Our sense of joy was infectious. We could not contain it in our hearts. We all stood and formed a circle around the Holy Bible. We held each other's hands and expressed our feelings. Our hand gestures and body movements became an expression of our joy. We sang a hymn of thanks and praise to Christ with gratitude as an expression of our unity. Our friends' disabilities did not hinder them from celebrating the peace of Christ. The peace of Christ brought us together and united us as a faith community that is grounded in trust, patience, kindness and understanding.

After our time for liturgy and catechesis in the sacred room, we continued enjoying the peace of Christ in our *agape*. The catechists used three tables to make one long one. They arranged the chairs. Marie placed the table mats. Andrea put the spoons on the table. Andrew prepared the pitcher of juice. Daniel added the cups. Leah set up the plates. Fred assisted in serving the food. Christ came to us through the Divine Word. Christ preached peace to us through the presence of our friends who were with us.

Christ's peace impelled us to serve one another during our preparation period, celebrating in a sacred room and sharing in *agape*. In that room, we got to know each other; we talked about things happening in our families, schools, workplaces and in society.

We experienced meaningful and transformative relationship, the friendship built on the peace of Christ. We were one body of Christ, regardless of age, gender, race, education, ability or profession. Each of us felt accepted and loved. It was our experience of mutuality in diversity and ability. The joy among us grew. We savored its beauty. It brought out goodness in us that shone upon our community. Together, we radiated the peace of Christ. With humility and confidence, we strove in our shared vocation to seek the grace of Christ—a glimpse of God's face.

Words of Saint Arnold Janssen
**"Yes, I want to love God,
as simply and humbly as a child."**

For reflection
- What has been my response to the gift of peace that Christ offers me in the Eucharist?
- How do I celebrate Christ's peace with the people in my life?

Have courage, wash one another's feet!

To wash ourselves is a basic and important skill we need in our lives. We were washed shortly after our mother gave birth to us. It's our common childhood experience. Growing up as children, we were incapable of washing our own bodies. Our parents spent time washing us regularly. Washing our body, as well as feeding and comforting us, is not merely our parents' responsibility but more importantly, it is an act of care and love for us.

My mother instilled in me the importance of washing my body daily. When I learned to wash myself on my own, I obediently took the responsibility of washing my younger brothers as they were growing up. It became one of our times for enjoying our childhood and establishing our brotherly love for each other. My responsibility extended eventually to washing dishes and doing laundry. Also, in our family livelihood of street food vending, I helped my parents as dishwasher in addition to bussing tables, resetting dining areas, washing dishes, flatware, pots and pans. I realized later on in my life that it was not just taking responsibility but more importantly it was serving people I love, my family.

I owe this discipline to my parents who taught me not only the skills of washing but also to uphold its value in my own life. It is something I am sharing with others. In our Divine Word Theologate community, washing dishes together after our meals is one of the ways that manifests our efforts to embody the interculturality that we acknowledge as our charism and that we cultivate as a community.

In the Gospel of John 13:1-15, Jesus washes his disciples' feet. Jesus acts as an example. He urges the disciples to do onto another as Jesus has done to them. Jesus did not allow himself to be served. He is the servant at his disciples' table.

Jesus' example goes beyond cleaning one's body, dishes or laundry. It tells us a deeper meaning about relationship and vocation in life with others. It is part of our call to become a loving, Christ-centered community.

It might be difficult for many of us to grasp deeply how Jesus served his disciples. Perhaps, we still feel incomplete even if we take Scripture courses or study Bible commentaries. Our minds might be filled with questions about Jesus' action. Probably like Peter we would be asking Jesus, "Are you going to wash my feet?" We long for a deeper and clearer understanding as we ponder Jesus' response to Peter, "What I am doing, you do not understand now, but you will understand later."

Many Bible scholars describe Jesus' gesture as a symbolic act of his saving ministry. What does this mean? It requires us to go beyond our head knowledge. We are called to seek growth in our understanding of Jesus and his actions. It's an invitation to become immersed in Christ's mystery.

My contemplation led me to recall several people whom I encountered at Saint Cajetan parish in Chicago, where I did my diaconal ministry. I felt Jesus' invitation to wash one another's feet.

Jesus' invitation of washing each other's feet goes beyond a household chore. It is not a self-service task. It is a call to selfless service for the sake of others who have been entrusted to us as our neighbors. To wash each other's feet entails the service of the Gospel and the service of Jesus' love for those who are like Peter.

I wondered about how to "wash the feet" of those who are like Peter, who pondered Jesus' desire, questioning Jesus' action, and misunderstanding Jesus' way. I recalled several people in our parish community. How do we follow Jesus' model of "washing other's feet," particularly for a son who feels anger toward God because of his father's illness; for a young son who is painfully in the middle of his parents' divorce; for a fearful daughter who asked me to bless a sacred object that she plans to give to her mom undergoing chemotherapy?

How do we wash the feet of a family who is mourning the loss of their loved one; or wash away a feeling of being marginalized in the parish community for being developmentally and intellectually disabled; or wash away the ignorance and arrogance of teenagers who lack knowledge about the significance of religious practices; or wash away the anxieties of parishioners who were worried about the potential closing of their well-loved parish.

As I offered my listening presence to the parishioners who shared their tribulations and sought understanding of their faith in Christ, I thought of Jesus' words, "if you understand this, blessed are you if you do it." Ministering as a deacon in our parish gave me the opportunity to enter into a relationship of service with the parishioners. Parishioners allowed me to serve them during their difficult times. Being given their trust made me feel like Peter when Jesus washed his feet.

We are directed to see washing others' feet through a different lens. In his book *No Man Is An Island*, Thomas Merton reminds us that "our love for one another must be rooted in a deep devotion to Divine Providence, a devotion that abandons our own limited plans into the hands of God and seeks only to enter into the invisible work that builds His Kingdom." To follow Jesus' act of washing his disciples' feet is to be open and willing to embody his new commandment that we love one another as he has loved us. To imitate Jesus, we must have the courage to be faithful, the courage to trust, the courage to love and serve others. In other words, we must wash one another's feet.

-------------------- 📖 --------------------
Words of Saint Arnold Janssen
"Go forward with full trust in God and resolve again to build up your life in holy humility."

For reflection
- What discourages me?
- In what ways do I fulfill Jesus' commandment to love one another as He has loved me?

To hold fast to the life that fosters faith, charity, and hope in time of pandemic

When we look back and think about things that have transpired during the pandemic, what thoughts and feelings come over us? The daily news about COVID-19 shows us the unprecedented and excruciating reality of our times; it leads us to ponder what kind of future lies ahead of us.

Many important events on my planner are now marked cancelled or postponed: long-distant races, the SPRED (Special Religious Development) ministry dinner dance fundraiser, the baptism of friends' children, the Easter Triduum celebration in the parish and graduation in May.

I had hoped that my family and friends could join me to celebrate the milestones of my vocation journey. To my dismay, the priesthood ordination has been postponed without knowing when and how to celebrate it. My inner fear gave rise to more questions about life and vocation. Does it still make sense to become priest for empty churches? Does faith have a future in an online church?

The worldwide pandemic has affected each one of us in various ways. All of us are urged to be morally responsible to take care of one another by abiding with the guidelines of social distancing, work from home, shelter in place, flatten the curve and enhance community quarantine.

The guidelines were implemented for our protection and safety; yet, it also makes us feel justifiably worried. Surely each one of us, depending on own story, feels something that no words can describe. It's an indescribable feeling that belongs to each of us alone. It is a feeling that I thought I would only encounter when I was close to the edge of death.

I brought my feeling of fear with me to my five-day ordination retreat–the only activity on my calendar that was not postponed or cancelled. During the first week of Easter, I spent this stay-at-home spiritual exercise contemplating the Resurrection narratives in the Scriptures.

I was drawn to the persons who witnessed the Risen Christ: the women hurriedly running away from the empty tomb; Mary Magdalene weeping at the tomb; the two troubled disciples walking on the road to Emmaus; and disciples who panicked, hid and were frightened when Jesus unexpectedly stood in their midst.

The apostles did not presume to inquire "Who are you?" when Jesus invited them to eat a meal with him after their fishing, and the doubting Thomas refused to believe in the Resurrected Jesus until he could see and feel the wounds received by Jesus on the cross.

At different levels, each of them was filled with fear. It was not the kind of fear that accompanied the complex emotions of anger, confusion and indifference. Their fear was the result of Divine Providence, a freely given gift from the Risen Lord that led them to and made them rely on their faith, love and hope.

I recalled the profoundly moving image of a shepherd taking care a flock when Pope Francis gave the special *Urbi et Orbi* blessing at Rome. He stood as a witness and servant of the

Good Shepherd Christ Jesus in a deserted St. Peter's Square with a steady rain falling.

He spoke to us through different means of modern communication; he led us to Jesus' question: "Why are you afraid? Have you no faith?" Pope Francis has proclaimed again and again the message of God's unconditional love and has urged us all "to reawaken and put into practice that solidarity and hope capable of giving strength, support and meaning to these hours when everything seems to be floundering."

While experts strive to collect and rely on data to understand how and why the pandemic is happening, we are tasked to reawaken our virtues of faith, love and hope.

We, the Church, the people of God, are missionary disciples. As frontliners, even though fearful, we must serve unselfishly to make sure that we do not become lifeless. We have a duty to make our Church community come fully alive.

We need to let the heart of the Risen Jesus Christ live in our hearts and in the hearts of all. Let the Easter mystery touch your life with the healing power of Jesus' love. Seek constant growth by putting into action the great work and teaching of Jesus. Free yourself from longing for only the passing things in life. Hold fast to the life Christ Jesus has given to us so that we come to the eternal gifts He promised all who follow him.

We do not know how long we will be in this situation. Faith, charity and hope make our waiting more worthwhile and meaningful. For us who are free from virus infection, let us be grateful and keep ourselves safe and healthy. At the same time, let us be merciful by nurturing and offering kindness.

Let us renew our family life, community life and prayer life. Let us grab our planners and organize concrete ways to live out our Christian life and vocation.

Words of Saint Arnold Janssen

"Everyone of us must say: I wish to please God the Lord through a faithful fulfillment of all that is my duty to do the whole long day."

For reflection

- What are the Gospel values that guide me during challenging times?
- How do I reawaken others' virtues of faith, love and hope especially in times of crisis?

Saint Arnold Janssen, SVD (1837-1909)

Arnold Janssen was born on November 5, 1837, in Goch, a small city in lower Rhineland (Germany). The second of ten children, his parents instilled in him a deep devotion to religion. He was ordained a priest on August 15, 1861, for the Diocese of Muenster and was assigned to teach natural sciences and mathematics in a secondary school in Bocholt. There, he was known for being a strict but just teacher. Due to his profound devotion to the Sacred Heart of Jesus, he was named diocesan director for the Apostleship of Prayer. This apostolate encouraged Arnold to open himself to Christians of other denominations.

Little by little, he became more aware of the spiritual needs of people beyond the limits of his own diocese, developing a deep concern for the universal mission of the Church. He decided to dedicate his life to awaking in the German church its missionary responsibility. With this in mind, in 1873 he resigned from his teaching post and soon after founded "The Little Messenger of the Sacred Heart." This popular monthly magazine presented news of missionary activities, and it encouraged German-speaking Catholics to do more to help the missions.

These were difficult times for the Catholic Church in Germany. Bismark unleashed the "Kulturkampf" with a series of anti-Catholic laws, which led to the expulsion of priests and religious and to the imprisonment of many bishops. In this chaotic situation Arnold Janssen proposed that some of the expelled priests could go to the foreign missions or at least help in the preparation of missionaries. Slowly but surely, and with a little prodding from the apostolic vicar of Hong Kong, Arnold discovered that God was calling him to undertake this difficult task. Many people said that he was not the right man for the job or that the times were not right for such a project. Arnold's answer was, "The Lord challenges our faith to do something new, precisely when so many things are collapsing in the Church."

With the support of a number of bishops, Arnold inaugurated the mission house on September 8, 1875, in Steyl, Holland, and thus began the Divine Word Missionaries. Already on March 2, 1879, the first two missionaries set out for China. One of these was Joseph Freinademetz.

Aware of the importance of publications for attracting vocations and funding, Arnold started a printing press just four months after the inauguration of the house. Thousands of generous lay persons contributed their time and effort to mission animation in German-speaking countries by helping to distribute the magazines from Steyl. From the beginning the new congregation developed as a community of both priests and Brothers.

The volunteers at the mission house included women as well as men. From practically the very beginning, a group of women, including Blessed Maria Helena Stollenwerk, served the community. But their wish was to serve the mission as Religious Sisters. The faithful, selfless service they freely offered and a recognition of the important role women could play in missionary outreach urged Arnold to found the mission congregation of the "Servants of the Holy Spirit," SSpS, on December 8, 1889. The first Sisters left for Argentina in 1895.

In 1896, Fr. Arnold selected some of the Sisters to form a cloistered branch to be known as "Servants of the Holy Spirit of Perpetual Adoration," SSpSAP. Their service to mission would be to maintain an uninterrupted adoration of the Blessed Sacrament, praying day and night for the Church and especially for the other two active missionary congregations.

Arnold died on January 15, 1909. His life was filled with a constant search for God's will, a great confidence in Divine Providence and hard work. That his work has been blessed is evident in the subsequent growth of the communities he founded: more than 6,000 Divine Word Missionaries are active in 63 countries, more than 3,800 missionary Servants of the Holy Spirit, and more than 400 Servants of the Holy Spirit of Perpetual Adoration.

Source: "SVD-Curia :: Our Founders." Accessed May 8, 2020. http://www.svdcuria.org/public/histtrad/founders/founders.htm

Acknowledgments

In one of his letters, Saint Arnold wrote, "I am not an expert writer. Often, I try to squeeze several topics into one letter as I cannot go into detail about every individual topic. Otherwise I would never finish my work." My feelings about writing deeply resonate with these words of our Divine Word Missionaries' founder.

I would like to express my joyful and grateful heart to many people who encouraged and guided me to publish a collection of stories and reflections about my experiences as a religious missionary. Without their support and wisdom, this book would not be possible.

I have to begin with a word of thanks to the Community members with whom I lived, namely to my formators and confreres with whom I journeyed at the Divine Word Theologate in Hyde Park, Chicago; to my SVD confreres in our Spain Province who accompanied me during my Cross-cultural Training Program, to our elderly and retired members in the Divine Word Residence in Techny, and to my confreres at East Troy, Wisconsin.

I will be forever grateful to the two persons who guided me closely and selflessly in doing this project by proofreading and editing the reflections I wrote during the past years. Thank you to Fr. William "Bill" Seifert, SVD, a companion and good friend with many responsibilities, for being a mentor who provided unceasingly the encouragement I needed to make this publication possible.

Likewise, I am deeply grateful to Theresa Carson, who inspired me and guided me in discovering my gift of writing that led to the completion of this book. Thank you for dreaming with me about what my book might come to be.

My heartfelt appreciation goes to Fr. Mike Hutchins, SVD, Fr. Quang Duc Dinh, SVD, and Mr. Tom Artz, for reviewing my reflections during the past years.

Thank you to Fr. Adam MacDonald, SVD, my vocation director and a good friend, for being a mentor since the time I entered the Society of the Divine Word, and and for graciously writing the introduction of the book.

Thank you to Fr. Jerry Orbos, SVD, one of the first Divine Word Missionaries I met. I admire him for his priestly ministry and especially for his preaching that inspires people by telling short stories grounded in God's Word. His published books, rooted in "moments spirituality," have truly influenced me in my desire to find life's meaning, to live with the Word of God and to encounter God himself in ordinary moments.

Thank you to Fr. Steve Bevans, SVD, my professor, mentor, confrere and a role model in our community. His teachings on contextual theology have helped me in seeking a better understanding of God's presence and love among the people I have encountered on my journey.

Moreover, I am thankful to all professors, staff, classmates and friends at Catholic Theological Union in Chicago. I am deeply grateful to those who gave feedback during the writing process, namely, Fr. Richard Fragomeni, who inspired me to be a minister with a great passion for proclaiming the Word and a commitment to serving the Word. His suggestion to include quotations from Saint Arnold made the book more meaningful and relatable to readers.

Sr. Dianne Bergant, CSA, for teaching me how to develop a manner of thought with the use of Scriptures that lead me to the constant deepening of theological reflection on life, which is an essential aspect in my ministry.

Sr. Maria Cimperman, RSCJ, for the course on the Spirituality of Religious Vows that I studied when I was a beginner in consecrated life. Her other two courses, the Theology and Practice of Ministry and the Introduction to Catholic Social Teachings, that have significantly influenced my reflections on lived experiences.

Prof. Anne McGowan, Ph.D., for her constant, thorough comments and encouraging feedback for every work that I did in class. She has been instrumental in awakening my ardor for the kind of liturgy that invites and leads a community to seek and find God's presence by giving praise and thanks.

Words are not enough to express my gratitude to Fr. James McCarthy, Sr. Mary Therese Harrington, SH, Sr. Suzanne Gallagher, SP, and our fellow catechists, our *friends,* and their families. The SPRED faith community has taught me that we must acknowledge the people with developmental and intellectual disabilities who live among us. They may not always be visible to us, but it is our duty to ensure that they are not forgotten and that they receive spiritual care.

Thank you to Joseph Richard Quane for being my honest, trusted, supportive and selfless adviser, critic, colleague, brother and friend.

I would like to acknowledge the significant role of my spiritual director Fr. James Gschwend, SJ, who accompanied and directed me to a better knowledge, understanding and acceptance of myself and my faith in God.

Thank you to Sr. Connie Schoen, OP, Fr. Guerric Ariel Llanes, OCSO, and Kitty Hartigan, who dedicated their time in reviewing the manuscript and writing their thoughtful testimonials.

I am deeply thankful to Fr. Steve Dombrowski and the parishioners of Saint Cajetan church in Chicago for allowing me to become part of their vibrant community and for sharing with me their gift of presence during my Diaconal ministry.

I would like to thank Sr. Lidia Kunze, SSpS, the members of the Missionary Sisters Servants of the Holy Spirit and the Holy Spirit Adoration Sisters for their unceasing support and prayers.

I am thankful for the support of Len Uhal, the director of our SVD Vocation Team, and his fellow vocation directors who untiringly provide guidance to those men and women who are discerning their call.

I will be forever grateful to my confrere and friend, Minh Anh Dinh, SVD, whose thoughtful insights have challenged me and led me to a deeper self-knowledge and stronger relationship with God.

Thank you to Carla Omania, Gaizel Adan and all my friends, former colleagues and students, whom I encountered throughout life's journey.

And especially to those with whom I began my journey, my family, for their love and prayers.

Indeed, to quote our founder Saint Arnold Janssen once again, "Gratitude is the foundation of our dedication to God, to do all that God wills."

Thank you very much!
¡Muchas gracias!
Maraming salamat!

Made in the USA
Monee, IL
19 August 2020